WINDOW FASHIONS

THE WORLD'S FAVORITE
WINDOW DECORATING BOOK

CHARLES RANDALL

For my wife, Patricia

Published in the United States by:
Charles Randall International
Las Vegas, Nevada
CharlesRandall.com

Cover photo: Krista Shugars, Pasadena, MD. Decorating Den Interiors, DecoratingDen.com.

Editor-in-Chief: Charles Randall

ISBN Paperback: 978-1-890379-65-0
ISBN: eBook: 978-1-890379-67-4

Library of Congress Cataloging-in-Publication Data

Names: Randall, Charles T., author.
Title: Window fashions : the world's favorite window decorating book /
  Charles Randall.
Other titles: Designer window fashions
Description: Second edition. | Anaheim, California : Charles Randall
  International, [2024] | Revised edition of: Designer window fashions /
  Charles Randall. Las Vegas, Nevada, USA : Charles Randall
  International, 2020. | Summary: "An exceptional guide to window
  coverings from the world's best-selling author on the subject.
Identifiers: LCCN 2024015522 (print) | LCCN 2024015523 (ebook) | ISBN
  9781890379650 (paperback) | ISBN 9781890379674 (ebook)
Subjects: LCSH: Windows in interior decoration. | Window shades. | Blinds.
  | Bedding.
Classification: LCC NK2115.5.D73 R353 2024 (print) | LCC NK2115.5.D73
  (ebook) | DDC 747/.3--dc23/eng/20240507
LC record available at https://lccn.loc.gov/2024015522
LC ebook record available at https://lccn.loc.gov/2024015523

INTRODUCTION

Reflecting on the incredible journey of the past thirty-five years, I am filled with pride. From its humble beginnings in 1986, the first edition of *Window Fashions* has evolved into the world's best-selling window decorating book, a testament to its enduring relevance and appeal.

In producing this new edition, I've aimed to pare down the technical information and make this book more user-friendly. This new streamlined edition continues the tradition of helping home decorating enthusiasts gain the knowledge to select the best window treatments for their homes and to help window decorating professionals provide all the information necessary for their clients to make the best possible decisions for their window-covering needs.

Is one picture worth a thousand words? Graphics have always stimulated the creation and communication of ideas. *Window Fashions'* value and usefulness are demonstrated by combining hundreds of photos and illustrations to display the vast selection of window treatments available.

Window Fashions stands as a beacon of practicality and effectiveness, guiding the design process for window treatments. For interior designers, this book is not just a valuable addition to their library but a trusted companion on their worktables and in the field. Its visual definitions of window treatments serve as instant communication tools, offering the best choices for any design situation.

The black line illustrations, strategically placed next to many photographs, are not just extra design options. They are sparks of creativity, showcasing variations in window covering treatments and introducing additional design elements that could elevate your initial design concept: tiebacks, jabots, rosettes, trims, banding, top treatments, and hardware, to name a few.

Get ready to be inspired! The new edition of *Window Fashions* is not just a book but a wellspring of ideas and creativity that will ignite your passion for window decorating. It's time to unleash your imagination and elevate your design concepts.

Charles Randall

CONTENTS

IMPORTANT QUESTIONS

While a basic window treatment will cover your bare window, it will not necessarily address other requirements you may have. Window treatments are not just about beauty but also privacy, sun protection, sound absorption, and more. Take some time to ponder the points listed below. When you sit down with a window treatment professional, he or she will ask your opinion on these topics. The better prepared you are to answer them, the more satisfied you will be with the result.

Existing Treatments

- What don't you like about your existing window coverings?
- Where is your window located?
- What is currently on the window? Is it easily removed? Do you wish to ret
- ain it in some capacity?
- Is the window non-traditional in shape? Do you have mismatched windows in the same room?

General Questions

- Have you given any thought to your budget? Do a little research online and check the "The Facts" boxes located in each chapter. Costs for treatments can vary considerably.
- Is this a window that will open frequently?
- Consider sound. If the room is noisy, would you like fabric at the window to help absorb the sound?
- Who lives in your home? Children, pets, adults, elderly? How might your window treatment affect those who dwell in your home?
- Are you interested in motorizing your window treatments? Consider motorization for any application, but you may need help operating in hard-to-reach areas or treatments.
- Would you consider employing the services of an interior or window treatment designer?

Qualities Needed

- How long do you expect to keep this treatment?
- Does it need to be moisture-resistant?
- What safety issues might you have; are small children or pets in your home?
- How important is energy conservation?

Time Frame/Installation

- How quickly do you hope to have your window treatment installed?
- Is this something you want to install on your own, or do you plan to hire someone?

Design Thoughts

- If you are completely redesigning your room, what is your design style? Do you prefer a soft, romantic look or a warm, traditional appearance? (Don't worry if you don't know — as you page this book, you may discover a style that's just right for you.)
- Is this window something you wish to emphasize — or deemphasize?
- Do you want to be able to maintain view (i.e., ensure privacy but still be able to enjoy sunlight)?
- Are there any architectural hindrances, such as window cranks, radiators, unsightly moldings, or light switches?

Finishes, Colors & Patterns

- Consider texture. How does a heavy velvet drapery compare to a sleek horizontal blind or a lace-like roller shade? Different textures make different statements.
- Patterns can add interest and depth to a poorly designed room or make it appear smaller and wider. How do you feel about decorative fabric patterns? Stripes? Checks? Florals? Small details?
- Color can tie together disparate elements in the room through a unifying tone or soften harsh lines. What kinds of colors do you like best? How will they fulfill the needs of your design scheme?

Cafe curtains are back! Another example of 'thinking outside of the box." Using two different hardware styles in the same room? It works perfectly. Custom window treatments are just that—custom. The only limit is the designer's and client's imagination. Decorating Den Interiors, .decoratingden.com.

How to Select Window Treatments

Function and style are the two most important considerations when deciding on window treatments. Knowing what you need the window treatment to do and what kind of feeling you want it to invoke will allow you more focus when making your purchase.

Function

First, decide what role you want your window treatment to play: purely aesthetic or a more practical purpose, such as creating privacy or blocking out the sunlight. Do you want to draw attention to a fabulous view or hide the spectacle of the unsightly home across the street? Create a list of the most important features your window treatment should have. These desired features will influence which types of window treatments may be appropriate. If you have small children or pets, you want to avoid window coverings with dangling cords or expensive silks that can become easily damaged. If you care more about the ornamental value of your window treatment, a drapery made of silk fabrics that puddle on the floor may be perfect for you. Roman shades or wooden shutters paired with draperies are excellent solutions for privacy.

Style

Once the more practical aspects of window dressings are solved, you can begin the fun part: using your creativity to beautify your home. Although you needn't stick with a theme when decorating, your new window treatment should complement the existing features of your home. Think about the mood you are trying to evoke. Use luxurious textiles layered in rich tones if you want your bedroom to appear sumptuous and exude warmth. If you want your office to appear chic and modern, go with simple lines and minimal detail. Window treatments can disguise flaws in a room or highlight features. If your living room has only a tiny window, you can make it appear larger by hanging your draperies higher and wider than the window. If a room lacks texture or warmth, you can use opulent fabrics or vivid hues to introduce these elements. To display a stunning ocean view, keep the window treatment simple yet elegant to draw the eye to the outside. And make sure the window covering stacks back from the window to expose the view. Most importantly, stay true to your style while being realistic about how your window treatment will perform inside your home.

Common mistakes to avoid:

1. Be careful when installing non-motorized or horizontal blinds or shades with cords over sliding glass or French doors. Because of the height of these windows, the strings become too long once the blinds are pulled up. Some shades and blinds (woven wood and wood blinds, for example) will stack so thickly at the top of the windows that you may have to bend down while passing through the doors. Exception: Mount treatment high enough to clear the window when raised. To do this, check the manufacturer's "stack-back charts." When raised, you will still have very long cords; therefore, it may be a bad idea altogether. Of course, the best option is motorized blinds to eliminate the cords, but most motors are slow, and you will have to wait quite a while for the blind to rise and lower. For most design choices, verticals or draperies are a much better idea for sliding glass doors. Never use a fabric tape measurer or attempt to "eyeball" a window's size. Always use a steel tape measurer to take measurements.

2. Don't forget to consider whether your window treatment will be visible from another room or outside the house, and account for those issues when choosing colors, textures, and shapes. Curb appeal is important.

3. Don't try to do it all yourself. Custom window treatments are custom; if you make a mistake, you cannot return the product. I highly recommend consulting a window decorating or interior design professional.

This wall of windows comprises five arched top sections in a three-sided bay. The client liked the ability to look out on the pool in good weather and wanted to cover the windows only partially. Fluer-de-lis patterned fabric in a subtle tone-on-tone satisfied the client's desire for a bit of New Orleans style. Two extra long panels were used to frame the window and the view. The arched shape at the top of the windows was maintained by using small medallions installed at the same angle, while a simple tie-back maximized the amount of light coming in from the tall windows. Heidi Sowatsky, St. Louis, MO. Decorating Den Interiors, decoratingden.com.

HIRING AN INTERIOR DESIGNER

Get Over Your Fears

IT IS A COMMON FEAR. Hiring an interior designer releases the design of your personal space into a stranger's hands. You no longer have control! They will enter your residence like a crazed designer, throwing their hands up about your style. Then, start submitting bills that would gag a billionaire. First, you don't want to live through the embarrassment of showing your current interior space to a professional. Second, you don't want to pay for something you don't like but are too intimidated to say so.

It's time to get over your fears and accept that you not only need a designer's opinion; you will probably save money, too. They won't measure 12 windows worth of blinds three times, place the order, and then discover the measurements are all wrong regarding installation. So, how do you reconcile yourself with hiring an interior designer and feel good about the process? It's called teamwork. Designers cannot read your mind — they need your help. Here's how to make it easier on yourself and get what you want.

- Look through the pages of this book, and perhaps my previous books, and apply some sticky note tabs to the pages with the window coverings that appeal to you. Soon, you will find a common thread running through your selected photos. Perhaps you'll find that all the rooms have a blue/green coloration. Maybe you're discovering that the photos you like are all sparsely decorated rooms. Now, show those photos when your designer asks, "What are you thinking about for this room."

- Interview prospective designers and review their portfolios. You may find that some designers specialize in an area of design that doesn't interest you. Another may not be a good personality match, while another may be the perfect match.

- Discuss your lifestyle, and don't hold back. If you have pets, children, if you smoke — all this will be taken into consideration. Complete the "Important Questions" on page 6 of this book and share it with your designer.

- Talk about fees upfront. Even though this project is personal, you are conducting business. Designers charge in various ways: by the hour, by a percentage of the project fee, and some with a flat fee. Then, get it in writing. Sign a contract that clarifies everything: time frames, cost overruns, designer's appearances on the job site, and how often you would like them to update you on the progress.

- Finally, talk about your needs. Don't say 'yes' to something unless you are certain it is what you want. Most designers will respect that greatly.

Is it time to accept that you need — and will come to value — the opinion of a qualified professional?
Interior Design is a creative profession; a designer is in business to serve your needs. Your happiness is their triumph!

This client's home has spectacular windows! They wanted some privacy but did not want to block off the view of the beautiful backyard foliage. The sheer pleated drapery gives the homeowners the privacy needed in this transitional family room and the option to enjoy the beautiful view of the backyard area. The two-story panels frame the tall windows, adding texture and interest and making a grand statement. Mary Elliott, Charlotte, SC. Decorating Den Interiors, decoratingden.com.

MOTORIZATION IS NOW AFFORDABLE!

BATTERY OPERATED OR HARD-WIRED? How to decide

ONE ITEM NOT DISCUSSED IN THIS BOOK, except for a few pages, is the topic of motorization.
It is common to be able to push a button and change a television channel or open a garage door. But have you considered the possibility of motorizing your window treatments? There are several kinds of motorization; which type is best for you depends on the window treatment(s) you are interested in motorizing and your budget. There are three types of possible applications: battery-operated, low-voltage, and hard-wired.

Battery-Operated

Although inexpensive to install, battery-operated systems require more regular maintenance than low-voltage or hard-wired. Batteries need to be changed occasionally. Consider that in areas where you may need to use a motor control most (such as a skylight system), you will need a high ladder to change the battery. If you are planning to motorize more than one treatment within a room, the good news is that battery-operated systems now offer "group" control options. The battery system is a good, affordable choice if you have an easy-to-access, lightweight treatment (like a pleated shade).

Low-Voltage

Low voltage is easier to install than a hard-wired system. A plug-in style that can easily operate a group of window treatments with a button. Ideal for "smaller" treatments (such as a group of blinds or shades), it is smaller and quieter than a hard-wired system. The downside to this type of electrical product is that it relies on its voltage, and longer wire lengths don't always deliver optimum efficiency.

Hard-Wired

With the greatest lifting, drawing, and tilting capacity, a hard-wired treatment is the most hardworking of the motorized systems. For example, you will need a hard-wired system to draw heavily lined and interlined heavy draperies. Hard-wired motors make it easy to accomplish. The downside to hard wiring is that it is best mapped out and installed in pre-construction, rather than afterward. Home automation is not a new concept, but the industry is fast-growing and ever-changing, offering new possibilities and levels of convenience. From shades that will lower at dusk to those that open and close while you are away on vacation to the ease of covering a skylight with a button, motorization improves life. Ask your designer about all the exciting new possibilities.

Consider that you can also ensure your privacy with motorization: no more standing in a dark window at night, closing your blinds.

The designer chose to frame this window with a soft pattern of fabric. The angled medallions lined up correctly with the ceiling, and soft white shades worked perfectly for both the transom and main windows – with the transom shades operating remotely. The window treatments had to accent and frame the chandelier softly, and the knob/medallion hardware was kept simple to enhance rather than detract from the room. Suzan Wemlinger, Milwaukee , WI. Decorating Den Interiors, decoratingden.com

DRAPERIES & CURTAINS

Curtains and draperies have enjoyed their decades of excess and floundered over times of pared-down minimalism. Consider all the wonderful uses for fabrics at the window: an interlined silk pinch pleat panel hanging stately in a period-style home, a simple sheer brushing lazily against a window frame, a dainty gingham checked café curtain decorating a kitchen. Fabric at the window softens edges, emphasizes (or de-emphasizes) architectural qualities and shortcomings, and provides a needed barrier between the outside elements and the inner harmony of the home.

My dream window treatments are honeycomb shades or shutters as the first line of defense against heat and noise. Then, subtle sheers soften the glare when the shades or louvers are opened, and finally, custom draperies with lining and a fabulous top treatment. Those are my dream window treatments—what are yours?

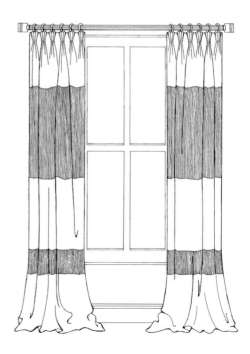

Left: These dramatic draperies are constructed from three fabrics in red, gold, and gray. To provide privacy, they traverse and are hung from antique brass hardware. Both areas in the principal suite are united with the same design. Barbara Elliott and Jennifer Ward-Woods, Stone Mountain, GA ., Decorating Den Interiors, decoratingden.com.

Right: Simple French pleated multi-fabric panels on decorative rods are great for a contemporary look. Stationary panels are adequate if puddled, but I recommend non-puddled for traversing draperies. Multi-arched flounced gathered and puddled panels on shepherd's crook decorative wrought iron rod.

Today's Curtains & Draperies

Today, as windows swoop to the ceiling — and even into the ceilings of many a home — fabric at the windows is an important statement. Indeed, some designers begin with the window treatment color palette before making decisions about anything else in a room. Decisions about draperies in the home fall into distinct categories: privacy (which also includes protection), physical and visual touch, light control, sound control, and color. Put these categories in order of preference; it will make a difference. For example, if you wish for privacy at night but have your heart set on a sheer only to diffuse light during the day, you may need to add another treatment, such as a cellular shade, to care for both needs.

Do not discount the emotion that fabric can bring to your home. The mood of an interior can be affected by the colors you choose: sunny versus somber, heavy fabrics versus light fabrics, casual versus elegant, or romantic versus businesslike. You will see examples as you page through this book. Examine the rooms. Find one similar in shape and scale to your own. Then, visualize how the treatments and fabrics will change the look of your space.

Right: A bohemian, eclectic, and natural style. The designer opted for banded draperies to offer vertical interest and a focal point. The space feels complete. Kimberly Paulus, Missouri City, TX., Decorating Den Interiors, decoratingden.com.

A special solution for the bank of windows was to create a truly one-of-a-kind custom window treatment that reflected the client's traditional style. Custom-shaped cornices with a light paisley pattern behind the drapery of each window. Topping the cornices are custom draperies with gold banding on each panel. Custom-made drapery hardware finishes this beautiful design. Sandy Kozar and Rachel Sheridan, Knoxville, TN., Decorating Den Interiors, decoratingden.com

The Facts: **Draperies & Curtains**

Advantages: Can camouflage bad woodwork and other architectural flaws; sound absorbent; can insulate, such as masking cold air leaks in windows. Also effective in blocking the sun's damaging rays, can be a room's focal point; if lined well, can offer privacy; softens the look of hard window treatments when used in combination; mount a drapery rod at ceiling level to enhance the height of a room; colored and patterned fabric can provide visual interest.

Disadvantages: Can be affected by moisture; color can fade when exposed to direct sunlight; improper dying can cause color transfer; can harbor dust and other allergic airborne entities. In general, sun and air pollution will work against fabrics, although some are more resistant than others. Drapery linings will offer good protection and lengthen the life of your drapery.

Cost: Inexpensive drapery panels can be acquired for as little as $20 at a local discount store—but if your goal is something more unique and perfectly suited for your environment, you should consider that cost may increase quite a bit. Quality, design, fiber type, linings, interlinings, embellishments and more will all factor into the price. Curtains and draperies are works of art, hand and machine sewn by talented workrooms.

Lifespan: Many variables will affect your draperies including sunlight, dust, humidity, and smoke fumes to name a few. On average, however, unlined draperies will last about four years; lined about six.

Most Appropriate Locations: Bedrooms, living rooms, dens, although fabric at the window has been long accepted in any location.

Care & Cleaning draperies on ones own can be tricky. Vacuuming with a soft brush is acceptable. Taking a drapery down to hang on an outside clothesline is fine (as long as you know how to rehang it properly) but depending upon whether your drapery is lined and/or whether it has decorative embellishments make cleaning draperies primarily a job for experts. Consult with your local dry cleaner, or employ an onsite drapery cleaner for best results.

These custom-colored block-style pinch-pleated side panels in blue and gray frame this beautiful window and enhance the view. Decorative tape accents the drapes and connects the colors. Black wrought iron rods hold the weight of this striking two-story window treatment. For functionality and to reduce UV rays entering the room, a Hunter Douglas motorized screen shade was installed. The remote control adds ease of use for the client. Mary Jo Long, Downingtown, PA. Decorating Den Interiors, decoratingden.com.

Good to Know: Fabrics

There are many fabrics today. In general, crisp fabrics lend themselves better to tailored treatments such as cornice boxes, pleated valances, draperies, and Roman shades, while soft, pliable fabrics are good for swags and cascades, Empire, and Kingston valances. Pliable fabrics also work well with balloon and cloud shades, London shades, and relaxed Roman shades.

Brocade: A rich and multicolored fabric. Typically used in upholstery but occasionally in draperies. Sometimes, it incorporates metallic threads as part of its all-over raised patterns or floral designs. It is traditionally created from a cotton background with rayon/silk patterns.

Burlap: Loosely constructed, this plain-weave jute fabric is often seen as housing for sacks of coffee beans or as backing on some flooring products. However, in recent years, this rough, coarse fabric has made its way into trendy interiors, reinvented as casual draperies — also, Jute.

Burnout: A technique used on many kinds of fabric but generally is a chemical solution applied to destroy a portion of the fabric while leaving other areas intact. An example would be burning a floral pattern out of the pile in a velvet piece while leaving the backing fabric intact. Burnout sheers are extremely popular, allowing light to filter through at various intensities.

Calico: This term is used primarily for simple curtains; this cotton fabric boasts small floral patterns (typically) on a contrasting background. An inexpensive fabric, calico is thin and not colorfast but crisp when ironed.

Canvas: A sturdy, plain weave cloth, this cotton or cotton/ polyester cloth offers a stiff and tailored yet casual look. Best for stationary drapery panels. Consider duck or sailcloth (lighter-weight canvas) if you require some draping.

Chintz: This cotton cloth offers bright colors, patterns, and floral motifs. Consider having this fabric lined if used in a window that receives direct sunlight, as the fabric will weaken, fade, and possibly rot over time. Sometimes, chintz is finished with a slight glaze to offer a polished look, although it will wash or wear off with repeated handling. It was prevalent in the 18th century, though it is still used frequently due to its lower cost and bright patterns for curtains or draperies.

Damask: A finer, thinner fabric than brocade, it nonetheless mixes shiny and dull threads to create beautiful patterns of high luster. They are crafted of silk, cotton, rayon, or linen. Its patterns are usually reversible, an example being a two-color damask in which the colors reverse depending on the side viewed. For draperies.

Dotted Swiss: A delicate, lightweight cotton fabric best suited for curtains. Small raised dots printed on either side of the fabric are the identifying detail. They are often woven into the fabric but, sometimes, applied to the surface (not as lovely).

Gingham: Usually seen in a plaid or checked pattern, gingham is a plain weave cotton fabric used often for café curtains and very light draperies. Typically, it is white with a one-color accent.

Jacquard refers to a weave more than a fabric. The Jacquard loom was invented in France in 1804 by Joseph Jacquard. Brocade, damask, and tapestry are some of the fabrics manufactured with a jacquard attachment, which permits separate control of each of the yarns processed.

Crisscrossed rod pocket panels swag gracefully across the arched window, enhancing but not hiding it.

The first design challenge was the morning sun's intense glare and heat, potentially damaging the leather sectional. The second challenge was to add warmth and softness to offset the abundant hard and plain surfaces. Dramatic, cord-drawn split-draw center, lined drapery pair three tiers high and flanked on each side by one-way cord-drawn lined panels. Heavy-duty decorative traverse hardware was needed to accomplish this dramatic design. Decorating Den Interior, decoratingden.com

Multi-arched flounced gathered and puddled panels on shepherd's crook decorative wrought iron rod.

Euro pleated panels with swag flags and jabots on decorative rods.

Grommet-topped drapery panels are held back with coordinating fabric tie-backs

Lace: A light, openwork cotton fabric typically used for sheers or curtains, its delicate mesh background consists of openwork designs. It is best to choose synthetic lace on window treatments to hold its shape when hanging.

Linen: This fiber is more robust and glossier than cotton; linen fibers are obtained from the interior of the woody stem of the flax plant. It is strong but needs to be pliable. It will wrinkle readily and is somewhat stiff. However, its sturdy and textured beauty can make for a more earthy style at the window in curtain or drapery form. Excellent sun resistance.

Matelassé: French meaning "padded" or "quilted," this medium to heavy double cloth fabric for draperies comes from silk, cotton, rayon, or wool.

Moiré: French meaning "watered," this silk, rayon, cotton, or acetate fabric has a distinctive wavy pattern on the surface that reflects light in the same way light reflects off the water.

Muslin: For casual curtains and draperies, cotton muslin can be fine to coarsely woven. It is typically used as liner fabric but has been the primary material. Coloration is neutral.

Nylon: Perfect for sheers, nylon is durable, washable, and inexpensive.

Organza (Organdy): This lightweight, crisp, sheer cotton fabric adds starch that will wash out. It will wrinkle quickly if crumpled or not finished with a wrinkle-resistant finish. It can take a variety of finishes and embellishments, including bleaching, dyeing, frosting, flocking, and more, for curtains and draperies.

Satin: With a matte back and a lustrous front, satin is available in many colors, weights, and degrees of stiffness. Traditionally, it is sometimes used at the window for evening and wedding garments and high-end bedding. It is expensive and slippery but used occasionally for drapery.

Silk: Silk is a natural filament, a product the silkworm creates when constructing its cocoon. There are many kinds of silk: tussah (wild silk, which is shorter and wider), shantung (raw and irregular), and dupioni (uneven and irregular threads), to name a few. Shiny and luxurious, it is a beautiful choice for drapery panels but will be affected by sun and water. It is expensive to line and interline this fabric at the window to protect it and lengthen its life.

Taffeta: A crisp fabric known best for its wonderful "rustle" sound, taffeta is a lustrous plain weave fabric usually made from synthetic fibers but sometimes silk. It is best used for draperies and has a crisp hand and much bulk.

Tapestry: Heavy and deliciously dense, the tapestry is often hand-woven and features elaborate motifs such as pictorials, floral, and historical scenes. While rarely used for curtains, tapestries are used as wall hangings and occasionally fitted with rod pockets to hang in front of a window. Today, the tapestry is more frequently constructed on a jacquard loom.

Toile: French for fabric or cloth, toile is best known as toile de Jouy, a finely printed design resembling a pen and ink drawing. Toile de Jouy is found primarily on cotton fabric and depicts romantic, idyllic scenes of pastoral countrysides, florals, and historical motifs.

Velvet: Plain and figured velvets are beautiful, soft, and best employed as drapery fabric. A medium-weight cut-pile fabric typically constructed of silk, rayon, cotton, or synthetics, its high luster and smooth hand create beautiful, graceful folds. Crease-resistant and inexpensive.

Voile: A lightweight, thin, semi-transparent fabric of cotton, wool, or silk. Voile is plain and loosely woven. Perfect for curtains or sheers, it gathers and drapes well.

This grand room is designed with a vibrant color palette of purples, fuchsia, goldenrod, and a touch of navy. The ten-foot-high windows are draped with jaw-dropping 125 inch stationary panels in fuchsia silk taffeta trimmed with an open-weave navy trim on the leading edge. The panels elegantly hang from acrylic rods accentuated with soft gold accents. Krista Shugars, Pasadena, MD. Decorating Den Interiors, decoratingden.com.

Curtains vs. Draperies

These two terms are not interchangeable, at least not on American soil. Consider that curtains are a less formal choice than draperies — they are typically less heavy, lighter, shorter, and more fanciful. Draperies utilize heavier fabrics, usually lined, to protect their beautiful colors and patterns from the sun's damaging rays. While both curtains and draperies may use decorative trims and tassels, a curtain typically uses smaller bands, braids, and trims. Drapery fabrics can handle heavy trims, tassels, and tie-backs easily.

Bolstering Your Fabric

There are many ways to keep your fabrics looking their best at the window. Always have your treatments lined unless you want the light to filter through. The lining gives draperies bulk protection and stability. Some unlined draperies can look like "ready-made" draperies, so use caution when deciding if they should be lined or unlined.

Here are the options:

Interfacing: Fabrics are used to offer support and give shape to the primary fabric. Some are designed and stitched to the primary fabric; others are fused through heat.

Interlining: An insulation of sorts to pad, stiffen, and protect the decorative fabric, as well as provide added insulation between the outside and the inside of the home. Interlining is sewn to the backside of the decorative room-facing fabric and then covered with the lining, which typically faces the street side of the window. Interlining is not seen but provides a great deal of protection and strength to a drapery.

Lining: A layer attached to the backside of the decorative room facing fabric or interlining to protect drapery fabric from sunrays and potential water damage from leaky windows. Adds bulk to a drapery.

Above and nex page: The designer completed this beautiful living room with bold and dramatic window treatments. The luxurious fabric of thRe draperies perfectly complements the modern shades of purple in the other accents of the space. The contemporary upper window tableau inserts provide an art piece in each window to set this room apart. Lisa Porter, Dallas, TX. Decorating Den Interiors, decoratingden.com

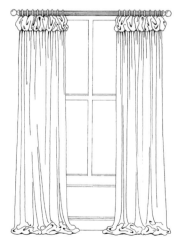

Puddled blouson drapery panels hung with rings offer casual elegance.

Grommet-topped panels make a simple, clean statement; fabric provides visual interest.

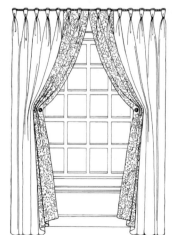

A small window is made to look larger by placing drapery panels higher and wider than the window.

Curtain & Drapery Styles

A short tutorial

Arch-top: A treatment for the specialty-shaped arch top window. A special frame is sometimes constructed with small hooks or pegs to shadow the curved area of the window. Loops are attached to this simple curved top treatment and hooked into place. It is a stationary treatment with the sides pulled out of the way.

Bishop sleeve: Tieback drapery panels bloused vertically at least once, most resembling a fancy garment's puffy sleeve.

Café curtain: Often designed as a two-tier treatment, café curtains are set at various heights for maximum privacy and light control, although usually at the top of a window and then again midway. Most café curtains can traverse if necessary.

Curtain: A simple treatment, typically unlined, usually stationary, or possibly hand drawn. They were usually hung on a simple rod.

Drapery: A heavier fabric/treatment often lined and usually able to open and close or stationary, it flanks either side of a window rather than hanging in front of it.

Festoon: Folded drapery fabric that hangs in a graceful curve from the top of the window, usually drawn upon cords. Festoon can also refer to a ribbon-tied garland balanced between two points (either side of a window), which drapes down in the center.

Flip topper: Typically, a flat, contrast-lined fabric panel that flips over a rod and is sometimes adorned with trim or beads to draw attention to its unique style. Flip toppers may also be cinched or triangulated in some way for added emphasis.

French pleat: A three-fold pleat found at the top of a drapery, also known as a pinch pleat.

Goblet pleat: Like a pinch pleat, only the top resembles a goblet's shape. Sometimes, the goblet is filled with batting to provide bulk or contrasting fabric for emphasis.

Hourglass: A permanently installed treatment attached at the top and bottom of a glass door or window, then pinched in the middle to create the hourglass shape. It provides some privacy but is mostly for decoration.

Inverted pleat: A reverse box pleat, also known as a kick pleat, conceals the extra fabric in the back. The pleat meets in the middle rather than is folded back at the sides.

Italian stringing: A historical way of drawing fabric in which diagonally strung cords attached to the back of the drape —about one-third of the way down — are manipulated to draw the drapery open and closed. For this to work, the top of the drapery must be stationary.

Knife pleat: Evenly spaced, tight, crisp, narrow pleats that run the length of the top of a drapery.

Pinch pleat: see French pleat.

Portiere: A drapery treatment that hangs in either a doorway or room entrance. Usually stationary, its main function is to soften and beautify an area. When operational, it can serve as a sound barrier between two rooms and alleviate drafts.

Rod pocket: This drapery style is a hollow tube-like sleeve at the top of a drapery (and sometimes the top/bottom of a curtain) that will accommodate a rod. The rod is attached to the wall or ceiling, and the drapery is suspended from it, and it can traverse back and forth with some difficulty. It is not recommended for traversing draperies.

Sheer: A light, see-through, or opaque fabric, never lined and often used for beauty and some sun/glare control, usually used in conjunction with draperies or modern shade treatment, such as cellular shades or blinds.

Stationary draperies: Usually hang to either side of the window and act as a decoration. It is not meant to provide protection from the sun or offer privacy.

Tab: A series of tabs at the top of the drapery, either a closed loop or a tie, in which a rod either slides through or is tied.

Tent fold: A drapery constructed to resemble an old-fashioned pup tent opening. The middle edge of the treatment is pulled back and secured, overlapping the rest of the drapery rather than pulling it all back. Will conceal much of the window, even when open.

The designer decided to start all over with this living room but kept some pieces that worked well with the new design. First, creating a symmetrical floor plan was achieved by clear entry into the living room. The space, with its pair of double doors and high-arched windows, needed to be highlighted. Identical, properly scaled sofas flanked the existing coffee table, providing symmetry, balance, and open entry to the living room. Next floor-to-ceiling window treatments with decorative edge banding emphasized the height of the windows, the view, and the grandeur of the room. Ottomans added extra texture, pattern, color, and seating. Lastly, the simple use of white paint brought out the architectural round ceiling design. All these details added up to one super dramatic room! Valery Huffenus, Ashville, NC. Decorating Den Interiors, decoratingden.com.

Left and above: With striking wallpaper on the ceiling, the designer balanced the room with custom rugs, draperies, decadent upholstery, tables, a mirror, and accessories, which continue the chinoiserie motif and style throughout the room. A show-stopping 42 inch square, commissioned painting makes this a special room indeed. Marni Sugarman, Riverdale, NY. Decorating Den Interiors, decoratingden.com.

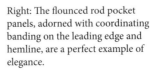

Left: Specialty swinging hardware allows for easy access to French doors. Coordinating fabric adds a nice touch. Hidden wands can be used to pull back the panels.

Right: The flounced rod pocket panels, adorned with coordinating banding on the leading edge and hemline, are a perfect example of elegance.

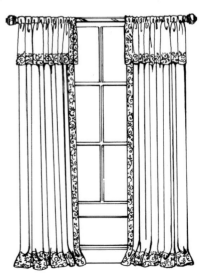

Single tone panels are set off by complementary decorative hardware

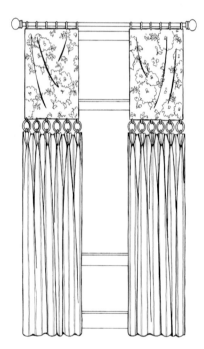

Stationary pleated draperies connected with rings under flat panels.

Left: The designer added draperies in updated traditional floral in soft gray and white, a band of lavender-washed linen at the leading edge and top of the panels. This offers a subtle pattern to the living room. Lightweight sheer drapes on a decorative gold traverse rod control the light and provide softness. The sheer drapes open to provide access to the adjacent porch. Cassy Young, Athens, GA. Decorating Den Interiors, decoratingden.com.

Inspired by the contemporary area rug, we chose lilac faux silk for simple but elegant drapery panels. The panels are hung on individual large shimmer gold medallions installed at an angle around the arched window. The panels were cut with an angled header and just three pleats - one for each medallion - and dressed on-site so that they lay nicely at both the top and the bottom. They are attached to the medallions with hidden zip ties. Heidi Sowatsky, St. Louis, MO. Decorating Den Interiors, decoratingden.com

The client wanted a design covering only part of the window to allow as much natural light as possible, so they chose stationary drapery panels. The treatment includes white silk panels with goblet pleats. The navy silk banding at the top and along the edge gives a Ralph Lauren look. To complete the design, the client chose acrylic and chrome rods and finials to add a touch of glamour. Kristin Williams, Fort Worth, TX. Decorating Den Interiors, decoratingden. com.

The designer worked with the client and provided multiple options to achieve the desired look. Rendering software and inspirational photos were used to communicate the concepts. Finally, the client chose navy blue velvet with a contrasting lining, giving the draperies extra flare and drama. With the addition of tassel trim and cording, a drapery masterpiece was created that the client loved! Mary Jo Long, Downingtown, PA. Decorating Den Interiors, decoratingden.com

This multi-functional family room was designed for a client's newly purchased brownstone in Boston's Back Bay area. The combination of modern and classic upholstery in gold, soft green, and neutral fabrics and light wood and metal case goods creates an inviting space for family time. Donna Smith, Walpole, MA. Decorating Den Interiors, decoratingden.com.

Fleur-de-lis tieback holders and tassel ties contain fringe-edged goblet pleated drapery panels with jabot accents.

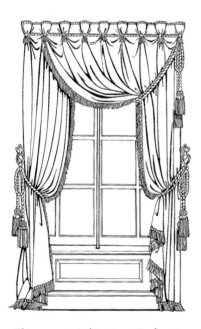

This asymmetrical treatment is a beauty with goblet pleats and bullion fringe. Note that the right-hand panel has top and middle tassel tiebacks, which balance and enhance its beauty.

Custom designed flags atop dramatic two-story draperies. Add shutters for privacy and light control, and you have a perfect designer window treatment. Cynthia Porche Interiors, cynthiaporcheinteriors.com

Left: The designer's CEO client needed an impressive family room to host annual company parties and provide comfort for a young family of five. The room was updated into a bright contemporary sitting area with a neutral, light but durable sofa and chairs, two-story geometric patterned draperies, navy blue velvet mid-century modern chairs, and turmeric-colored pillows for added drama. The U-shaped layout, with light wood, marble occasional tables, and chrome lamps, adds polish. Lynne Lawson and Laura Outland, Columbia, MD. Decorating Den Interiors, decoratingden.com.

Above: The high ceiling and Palladian windows made this formal living room a design challenge. The inspired solution was to bring down the ceiling visually to create a more intimate space, accomplished by using a dark navy horizontal fabric band placed at the bottom of the draperies to draw the eyes downward. The medallion holdbacks tie in with the Venetian style windows. The colors of the room, in addition to the ceiling treatment, enhance the room's grandeur while, at the same time, help to lower the height without adding too much vertical weight. Mimi Wilson, Bristow, VA. Decorating Den Interiors, decoratingden.com.

The windows are dressed in two layers. Softly pleated sheers provide sun control while the panels are hung stationary on the sides. The fabric for the goblet pleated panels is gold embroidered linen. The soft pattern adds texture without too much movement. Double chrome rods accented with crystal finials complete the ensemble. Barbara Elliott and Jennifer Ward-Woods, Stone Mountain, GA. Decorating Den Interiors, decoratingden.com.

Arched Bishop sleeve panels with rosettes and rope tassels.

Close up of drapery jewelry opposite page

Two-layer treatment with sheers over solid silk lined and interlined draperies add opulence and drapeability. Sheer swags hung from custom-designed hardware on both the top and side crowns. Crystal drapery jewelry (see close-up opposite page) used to coordinate with crystal chandelier.
Susan Gailani, ASID Allied, Gailani Designs Inc., gailanidesigns.com

Sweeping views and warm textures abound in this transitional great room. Two-story windows and stationary floor-to-ceiling two-finger pleated custom-designed draperies with woven wood shades fill this grand room with stunning custom window treatments. The mixed-use of plaid and solid fabrics in a board-mounted design creates a visual delight in this home. Marva Don Card, Fort Denaud, FL. Decorating Den Interiors, decoratingden.com.

Above: The adjacent room theme is carried over to this dining area. A beautiful design is made of stationary pleated draperies with coordinating banding matching the Roman shades.

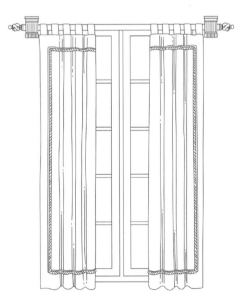

Tab top panels with contrasting banding. Custom rendering by DreamDraper® design software, dreamdraper.com © 2009 Evan Marsh Designs, Inc.

Flat panel/Athena style draperies with applique and bullion fringe hems hang gracefully on a decorative rod.

French Country toile in an updated botanical print with birds sets the tone for this office window treatment. The panels are installed on boards, so they don't distract from the white shutters that extend the full length of the window and its transoms. Heidi Sowatsky, St. Louis, MO. Decorating Den Interiors, decoratingden.com

Unabashedly eye-catching, arched Bishop sleeve drapery panels with rich coloration, coupled with over-scale tassels, are entirely sophisticated.
Decorating Den Interiors, decoratingden.com

A historic Craftsman living room gets a pulled-together update, starting with a gorgeous velvet green tufted sofa. Chairs have peek-a-boo backs and interesting accent tables, which make the space great for entertainment. The soft greens and neutrals are repeated in a soft wool rug. The tall ceilings are highlighted with long green leafy patterned drapery panels and a white and black chandelier. The built-ins and fireplace are carefully styled with the room's and home's accent colors. Decorating Den Interiors, decoratingden.com.

Charleston, South Carolina, verandas inspired this sunroom décor in this large, octagonal sunroom. It has a faceted glass ceiling and fretwork throughout. The designer persuaded the clients to do six grass-green, faux silk, interlined, stationary panels to accentuate angles and draw the eye up and out. Each edge has a wide, sophisticated grey and white flat trim. Panels are strategically mounted on hidden custom-made traverse rods (2 per angled panel) around and within the fretwork.

Arched pleated and trimmed draperies on curved wrought iron rods with matching tableaux grille in the top window. Designer: Gillian Wendel, Workroom: Bonnie Sides, Photo: Brandy Stoesz.

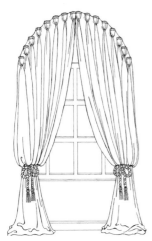

Arched goblet pleated draperies with rope ties.

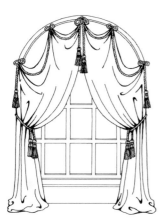

Instead of hiding the shape of this grand window, a drapery treatment accents its graceful arch. Tassel detailing is an inspired choice.

Intriguing drapery hardware provides the focal point for this arch-top window; drapeable fabric provides a soft accent.

These delightful arched windows are embraced with matching custom curved drapery hardware. Le Fer Forge Drapery Hardware leferforge.com

Left: Self-lined, flat, sheer blue panels were tied onto a custom iron "birds on branch" rod with ties threaded through buttonholes in the panels, allowing for a small droop between ties. The panels were pulled back gently with iron bird tiebacks.
Designer, Susan Keefe, CID.

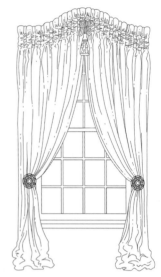

Arched goblet pleats with medallion holdbacks.

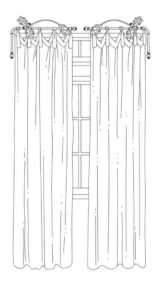

Tie top on swing arm rods.
Both illustrations: Custom rendering by DreamDraper® design software, dreamdraper.com
© 2009 Evan Marsh Designs, Inc.

Wide width embroidered sheer fabric was used "up the roll" to create maximum fullness - shirred at the top, overlapped and stapled onto a large wood rod.
Designer, Susan Keefe, CID

Ring top draperies with simple braid tiebacks.

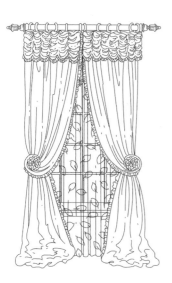

Sheer undertreatments are enhanced with puddled ring top drapery panels and gathered valance. Both illustrations: Custom rendering by DreamDraper® design software, dreamdraper.com © 2009 Evan Marsh Designs, Inc.

Above: The room's backdrop is soft gray, and varying shades of gray are used in the furniture, floor coverings, and art to provide added dimensions. The furniture's lines give the space an eclectic and modern vibe. The wow factor came from the chandelier and mixed metals in the accent pieces. Lisa Porter, Dallas, TX. Decorating Den Interiors, decoratingden. com

Left: Flat-panel draperies attached with wrought iron medallions gracefully swag across this magnificent window. This treatment matches perfectly with the inviting room décor; a delight to behold. Cynthia Porche Interiors,

cynthiaporcheinteriors.com

Stationary panels with banded, ruffled tops make an elegant statement. Custom rendering by DreamDraper® design software, dreamdraper. com© 2009 Evan Marsh Designs, Inc.

Puddled draperies with swag embellishment are hung slightly lower to expose the decorative glass. Custom rendering by DreamDraper® design software, dreamdraper.com © 2009 Evan Marsh Designs Inc.

These panels are hung from chrome rods with crystal finials. Gray faux silk was used for the panels and accented with orange silk. Barbara Elliott and Jennifer Ward-Woods. Stone Mountain, GA. Decorating Den Interiors, decoratingden.com

For the windows, 2" wood blinds were installed for privacy. Drapery panels were constructed from an orange sateen and gray fabric with crystal highlights. Chrome hardware and crystal-accented hardware complete the look. Sandy Kozar and Rachel Sheridan, Knoxville, TN, Decorating Den Interiors, decoratingden.com

Silk and satin color-blocked draperies separated by golden fabric are a match made in heaven! Add a decorative rod with beautiful complimentary finials, and you have a designer window treatment. Barbara Elliott and Jennifer Ward Woods, Stone Mountain, GA. Decorating Den Interiors, .decorating-den.com

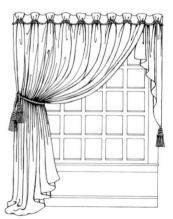

Arched goblet-pleated draperies with jabot accent are pulled back with Italian stringing. Note the pretty braid and fringe trim.

Triple blouson tops on the drapery panels draw the eye with their unique beauty.

A goblet-pleated drapery treatment is enhanced with a small cascade on the right-hand side: tassels and interesting details.

The designers bathed the walls in beautiful navy paint to create a Wow effect. Then, they added a beautiful silk jacquard with purple accents to increase the color palette for the window treatments. Barbara Elliott and Jennifer Ward-Woods, Stone Mountain, GA. Decorating Den Interiors, decoratingden.com.

TOP TREATMENTS

When your heart says, "beautiful window covering," but your room says, "not enough space!" The solution is a stunning top treatment. From a soft swag dipping gracefully across a window to the hard edges of a wood cornice, the function of a top treatment is to provide beauty to a home, hide the mechanics of combined window treatments, disguise architectural flaws and also to emphasize and draw focus to a window. By itself or as beautiful punctuation, valances, cornices, and swags (the lion's share of the top treatment category) are excellent choices when dressing a window.

Left: Long embroidered drapery panels floor to ceiling and shorter panels on the sides draped back helped to unify the top windows, which are wider than the bottom windows, into one cohesive treatment. Motorized solar shades added to the large bank of windows addressed the needed midday sun control and heat control and were tucked neatly into a small headrail that blends with the trim work when not in use. The window treatments help soften all the stonework in the room and complement the height. The result: A stunning window treatment! Kathy McGroarty, Millsboro, DE. Decorating Den Interiors, decoratingden.com

An arched quilted cornice box is mirrored on the deep bottom hem of the pleated draperies.

Today's Top Treatments

Today, there are almost unlimited choices for top treatments, allowing for more creative exploration for the designer and workroom due to their smaller scale. "Theme" cornices are often a favorite in children's rooms: baseball pennants at the top of a cornice or ballet slippers are used as a decorative element to secure the corners of a small swag. A single handkerchief swag will punctuate a bathroom window, and an elaborate padded and upholstered cornice will add beautiful emphasis to sumptuous draperies.

A small buffalo check was chosen to coordinate with the chairs in the seating area, rug, and print color. The unique, custom hardware was selected for the client because of the brackets with the birds on them; leaf finials were added to enhance the feel of nature. The antique brass finish was selected to coordinate with the fabric and provide contrast so the hardware would stand out. A pole-mounted tab top Queen Ann valance with contrast banding and premade micro-cording on the bottom scallop was the best design to avoid overwhelming the treatment. Sandy Kozar and Rachel Sheridan, Knoxville, TN. Decorating Den Interiors, decoratingden.com

Good to Know: **A Few Top Treatment Terms**

What's the difference between a cornice and a lambrequin? A valance and a pelmet? Here's a look:

Balloon: A soft fabric valance that is billowy and lush, drooping in graceful, looping folds across the top of a window. It is also known as a cloud, though the shape varies slightly.

Box pleat: A flat, symmetrical fold of cloth sewn in place to create fullness, spaced evenly across the top of a drapery. For example, the fabric can be folded back on either side of the pleat to show a contrasting fabric.

Cascade: A zig-zagged or cascading-shaped fabric falling gracefully from the top of a drapery or top treatment. Depending on the size and shape, it can also be called a jabot.

Cornice: A rigid treatment that sometimes serves as a mask for holding attached stationary draperies, hiding various window treatment hardware, or even masking architectural flaws. Constructed of a chipboard-style wood or lightweight material, over which some padding (usually polyester fill) is added, then covered with a fabric of choice and finished with trim. Cornices fit across the top of a window frame and can be a terrific focal point, usually mounted outside a window frame.

Jabot: A decorative, stationary panel used in tandem with a swag (festoon) and also known as a tail.

Lambrequin: An extended version of the cornice, the lambrequin, not only fits across the top of the window frame but also extends down on either side, resembling legs. Shaped or straight, this three-sided piece is created in much the same manner as a cornice but is typically more elaborately decorated. See the first page of Top Treatments: Cornices, for example.

Pelmet: The British term for top treatment.

Rosette: Fabric gathered into the shape of a flower or something similar. Typically placed at the top right and left corners of a window frame to accent an existing treatment, such as a scarf or drapery panel.

Scarf: A single, lengthy piece of lightweight fabric that wraps loosely around a stationary rod or loops through decorative brackets on either side of a window frame.

Swag: There are many kinds of swag top treatments. The prevalent styles are basic pole swags or board-mounted swags.

Valance: A simple to elaborate treatment, valance is a piece of decorative fabric usually hung from a rod, a piece of decorative hardware, or aboard. Valances can take on many shapes: poufed, scalloped, pointed, arched, and rectangular, and can also be pleated or gathered.

The scalloped fabric shade's trim is echoed in the soft swag and cascade. Note, too, that this is a four-part treatment—both sheer and regular drapery panels are employed.

The Facts: **Top Treatments**

Advantages: Perfect for areas that cannot accommodate larger treatments. Above kitchen sinks and limited space areas. A top treatment can hide architectural flaws, such as windows at different heights. They can also soften hard window treatments and introduce a beautiful focal point to any room.

Disadvantages: Not particularly useful for privacy or sun control. They can gather dust due to their stationary nature. They can overpower a small window if not designed carefully.

Cost: Top treatment costs can vary significantly. Wood or wrought iron cornices will be more costly than a padded fabric-covered cornice. A swag and tail treatment is usually more costly than a scarf top treatment.

Lifespan: 7-15 years.

Most Appropriate Locations: Anywhere a window needs softening, but space is at a premium. As always, keep fabric away from areas of extreme moisture to cut back on issues of mold growth and fabric discoloration.

Care & Cleaning: Depending upon the type of treatment, you may be able to vacuum or dust the window, remove any dust, or remove and have it cleaned professionally. Refrain from attempting to wash your top treatments conventionally. Swag and tail treatments are usually more costly than a scarf top treatment.

Below: Green silk scarves swag gently over decorative poles to soften the window area without impeding the view. It is their simplicity that is so appealing. While there is certainly room for drapery panels — or multi-layered treatments for that matter — the simplicity of the treatment is pleasing to the eye.

Two-story draperies are always impressive. Adding swags and double cascades make the room go from impressive to extraordinary. Designed and made by Custom Drapery Workroom, Inc., draperyavenue.com

Top Treatments: **Swags & Cascades**

As diverse as they are versatile, swags and cascades can assume many roles, taking the lead role in a dramatic and eye-popping capacity—or perhaps just a supporting role or bit part. At its most subtle, a swag and cascade combination can take shape as it winds itself around a pole in a slouchy and casual way; for a more involved installation, look to a swag accompanying drapery panels. No matter how it's installed, however: board mounted, pole mounted, multi-layers, or just a single, this time-tested top treatment is certain to make a statement.

Left: Short, narrow windows were corrected visually with the placement of an unusual arch top decorative rod, which adds height and drama. The blend of pink and blue can sometimes be polarizing, but this combination exudes style and elegance, with the pink banding allowing the treatment to distinguish itself from similarly colored walls. Notice, too, that the vine-like scrolling on the hardware echoes the floral fabric motif.
Emily B. Walser, ASID, photograph courtesy of Dustin Peck, Dustin Peck Photography

Above: This Scandinavian-style scarf treatment is casual and easy. Also appreciated is the use of complementary fabrics, rather than using the same fabric for both doorways. ADO-USA
Right: Sheer handkerchief swags with long, flowing tails accentuate the tall window wall without detracting from the view outside. Kenny Greene, Greene Designs

Multiple scarf swag treatments accent the window without over-powering it. Custom rendering by DreamDraper® design software, dreamdraper.com © 2009 Evan Marsh Designs, Inc

This complicated bay window needs accuracy and precision for the top treatment to flow seamlessly. Designed and made by Custom Drapery Workroom, Inc., draperyavenue.com

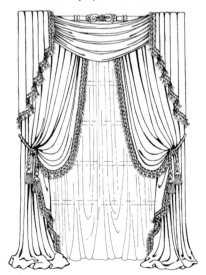

Open swag and cascades with trim on a decorative rod, tiebacks, and tassels finish this extraordinary treatment.

Pole-gathered swags with decorative knots, cascades, and trimmed panels.

Goblet pleated panels with swag flags and small cascades.

Unique and creative ideas for top treatments open an array of luxury. Designed and made by Custom Drapery Workroom, Inc., draperyavenue.com

Rod pocket pole swag and gathered drapery with trimmed flounce.

Gathered linear swags over traditional overlapping swags with stacking cascades make for an elegant and expensive treatment. Finished with rosettes and tassels.

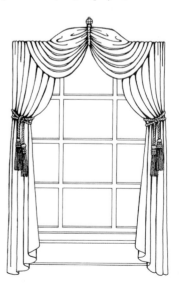

Large tassels dangling from braided tiebacks create visual interest in this simple but stunning treatment.

Regal blue and gold fabrics made for a foyer with double light sheers to complement and control sunlight. Designed and made by Custom Drapery Workroom, Inc., draperyavenue.com

Unique top treatment for the master bedroom, the fullness made it cozy ready for the Chicago winters. Designed and made by Custom Drapery Workroom, Inc.,.draperyavenue.com

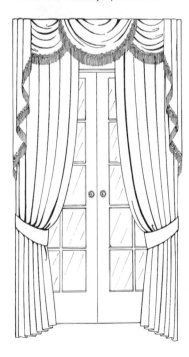

Board mounting swags and cascades with tied-back panels.

Sheer under treatment, swags, cascades, and panels.

Fabric hangs in shabby chic swag and cascade style, layered over lush, puddled stationary drapery panels.

Turban-style swags grace these contrasting drapery panels. These swags are hybrids of sorts: they are part swags, and part cornice boxes with their vertical wood support on each side and above. I love it when designers combine two different style window treatments into one genuinely creative design. Decorating Den Interiors, decoratingden.com

This drapery and swag style is one of the workroom's favorite and ultra popular designs. Designed and made by Custom Drapery Workroom Inc., draperyavenue.com

Linear swags and stacked cascades. draperyavenue.com

Swags and cascades over Austrian shade. draperyavenue.com

Top Treatments: **Valances**

Top treatments, such as this versatile inverted box pleated valance, have the wonderful capability to be infinitely casual or completely elegant. Take the feminine cloud valance, for example; it will step into a supporting role alongside an elegant set of draperies or a modest vertical or sheer shading shade. Other styles will command a room, drawing the spotlight upon themselves so all may enjoy their standalone beauty. From the most petite bathroom window to a large picture window, a soft valance may be the answer to any window dressing question.

Left: An inverted box pleated valance with luxurious white cotton fabric accented with decorative sun-inspired banding near the bottom of the valance, and the leading edge of the drapery is an inspired choice: a beautiful combination of formal and modern. A closer look reveals the coordinating welt and tassels atop and below this fabulous drapery treatment. Add a scalloped Roman shade, and you have a truly designer treatment. Decorating Den Interiors, decoratingden.com

Above: The clean lines of the cream flat-panel valances with decorative teal banding add elegance to the room and flow nicely with the drapery panels in this dining area. Mary Elliott, Indian Trail, NC. Decorating Den Interiors, decoratingden.com

Right: The window treatments in this bedroom transform it from cumbersome to airy and grand. The delicate sheers soften the light for a romantic aesthetic. The draperies accented with light metallic embroidery and the custom window inserts create a dramatic look. The prominence of vertical lines accentuates the space's architectural details. Kathy Potts, Forest, VA. Decorating Den Interiors, decoratingden.com

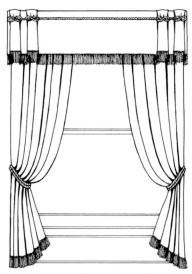

A soft cornice with simple side pleats enhanced with bullion fringe and tiebacks.

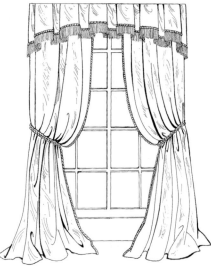

A scalloped ring top space pleated valance with small tassel fringe complements the pleated drapery panels—which can easily be released from their hold-backs to provide privacy.

Left: At the heart of this project is a captivating black, white, and gray hexagon tile, satisfying the client's desire for timeless flooring with added interest. Off-white cabinets and a cloud-gray desk area create a chic kitchen space. Shimmering Cambria quartz, gleaming subway tile, and mother-of-pearl backsplash add elegance. Brushed gold accents, a marble dining table, and blue-gray velvet chairs contribute warmth and sophistication. Plantation shutters provide a classic look, while cohesive window treatments tie the design together with black and blue accents. Bonnie Pressley, Fort Worth, TX. Decorating Den Interiors, decoratingden.com.

On the walls of windows, the designer created faux Roman shades in striking, golden flame stitch wovens. Then, a traditional marigold rug was selected and topped with a farm table and chairs featuring rattan backs. The light fixtures in this room, like the jewelry, make a statement with rattan and wood beads; they complete this inviting dining space. Marni Sugerman, Larchmont, NY. Decorating Den Interiors, decoratingden.com

Townhome dining, with a custom-designed banquette and lighting. A walnut table anchors the small space with cane-backed seating. Abundant light is filtered through plantation shutters. A chair covered in a classic crewel balances the room. Original still-life paintings are the star of the show. Nancy Gillespie, Louisville, KY. Decorating Den Interiors, decoratingden.com

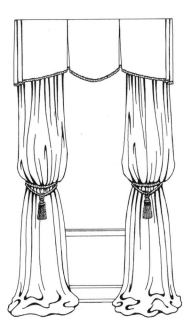

A box pleated valance atop Bishop sleeve panels accented with tassels.

An offset arched non-pleated valance with an offset triangle flag is an unusual twist. Pleated stationary panels complete the treatment.

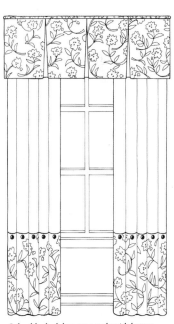

Color-blocked drapery panels with button accents complement the inverted box-pleated valance.

The client wanted this main bedroom to be serene, so we added remote-controlled room darkening roller shades as a starting point. Then, we added drapery side panels with embroidered geometric designs on chrome rods. Finally, we added stagecoach valances with tone-on-tone vine pattern fabric,

bead trim, and white ties and buttons. Diana Apgar, Middletown, OH. Decorating Den Interiors, decoratingden.com

Above: Queen Ann style valance with jabots work perfectly in the bay window. Note how the jabots/tails line up with the bay angles. Piping along the top of the valance adds extra detail. Decorating Den Interiors, decoratingden.com

Left: This gorgeous valance was created with tab tops hanging on a golden decorative rod with beautifully matching finials. Custom shaped bottom with trim adds the drama. Add striped silk draperies and sheers and you have a timeless window coverings masterpiece. Tonie Vanderhulst, Wellington, FL., Decorating Den Interiors, .decoratingden.com

This graceful treatment is created using a non-pleated valance and adding Maltese cross jabots and ties.

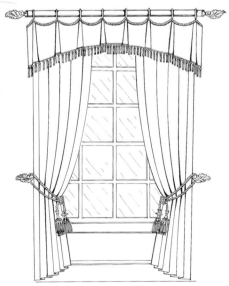

A scalloped ring top space pleated valance with small tassel fringe complements the pleated drapery panels—which can easily be released from their holdbacks to provide privacy.

Top Treatments: **Cornice Boxes**

Whether alone or as an accompaniment to an existing window treatment, cornices can be a wonderful addition to any home decor. Though they are a permanent window treatment usually installed snugly next to a window frame, a cornice box is anything but sedentary. Situated atop a tall window, an intricately carved cornice box can transport the room to a time when kings and queens lived in opulence. Conversely, a shaped cornice above a child's window adorned with a favorite animal or icon can contribute to a playful theme in a big way. Upholstered cornices provide a classic topping for windows of any size, making an excellent over-treatment for draperies, vertical blinds, or sheer shadings. The cornice is constructed of a wooden frame that is padded and upholstered in a decorative fabric and is usually finished with piping on the top and bottom edges.

Right: The curved chaise sectional is an invitation to relax in performance fabric. Soft teal, solid, and cut velvet fabric pillows knife-edge paired with motion wall hugging swivel recliner neutral gray—stylish bench with a cerused linen finish and small-scale pattern for extra seating. Custom shelves display accessories and artwork. The handmade abaca chandelier gives ambiance to this transitional design. Heidi Sowatsky, St. Louis, MO. Decorating Den Interiors, decoraitingden.com.

Left:These Moroccan inspired lambrequins are a perfect choice for this two-story breakfast nook. Note the abundant floor pillow seating in keeping with Moroccan dining tradition. Motorized flat Roman shades in aqua add the final flair to this enchanted space. Private residence, Bel Air, California, Jeanne Candler Design, jcandlerdesign.com.
Photo: Charles Randall

Right: The designer presented the client with a beautiful Carole white faux silk fabric with a coordinating trim that would accent the wall color. A shaped cornice with a black and white toile fabric works perfectly with the Asian theme in the room. The client was ecstatic with the window treatments and now enjoys using the dining room. Mary Jo Long, Downingtown, PA. Decorating Den Interiors, decoratingden.com

Sometimes, the fabric pattern will help you choose the cornice box design. Note that the checkered pattern is lined up with the dropping sides of this custom-shaped cornice.

Above: The challenge was to provide window treatments that would accentuate the grandness of the room. The designer used a transitional beige and red damask pattern in a cotton poly blend for the pinch pleat panels to accomplish this task. The panels were installed under custom mini cornices padded with extra batting to give them more substance since they were so high up. This combination greatly helped with the acoustics and added warmth to the room. Mary Jo Long. Decorating Den Interiors, decoratingden.com

This designer creation consists of an arched cornice under arched inverted box pleated drapery panels. The nail heads securing the panels and wrought iron grill adds extra interest. Nola Shivers and Linda Tully, Nixa, MO. Photographer Jeremy McGraw. Decorating Den Interiors, decoratingden.com

This window treatment design was developed to draw the eye up and enhance the window by softening all the lines and angles. The beautiful embellished sheer fabric flows softly from custom cornices that top the windows at different heights. Antique silver Tableaux faux iron was overlaid on charcoal custom cornices. Custom cornices are notched out on one side to fit snugly over the trim and return neatly to the wall on the other return side of each cornice. All parts of this dramatic window treatment work together to make this the focal point as guests enter this room. Cathi Lloyd, Sylvania, OH. Decorating Den Interiors, decoratingden.com

This fantastic design employs white cornice boxes trimmed in navy and top off the two-story lime green drapery panels. Look closely and see the large jewel nail head that provides bling in the center of the X on the cornice. Attention to detail makes a big difference when it comes to creating a fabulous window covering. Heidi Sowatsky, St. Louis, MO. Decorating Den Interiors, decoratingden.com

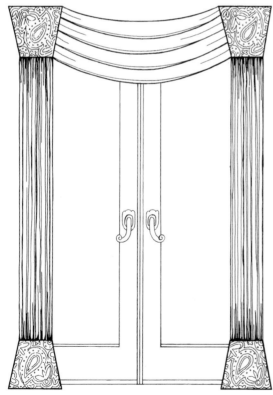

Trillian cornices at top and bottom flank the doorway and hold the single swag at the top and the shirred vertical fabric treatments, too.

Upholstered trillian cornices accentuate the view; swagged fabric in between vertically softens, puddled drapery enhance

WINDOW COVERING COMBINATIONS

Who says you can't have the best of both worlds? When one window treatment isn't enough, exploring the beauty and flexibility of combination treatments is the perfect way to proceed. Typically, modern (hard) window treatments (such as blinds or shutters) are combined with stationary drapery panels… fabric shades… a top treatment…or whatever your heart desires. Indeed, the hard treatment sometimes stays, with the soft treatment changing as often as the homeowner wishes.

Left: This fabulous eye-pleasing design was created by selecting a geometric fabric in black and white for the window treatment and hanging it on a black wrought-iron rod to frame the windows. Barbara Elliott and Jennifer Ward Woods, Stone Mountain, GA. Decorating Den Interiors, decoratingden.com.

Goblet-pleated Italian strung drapery panels cascade to the floor. A flat-panel Roman shade underneath provides privacy and sun control.

Today's Combinations

Today, combinations come in many configurations, but at their best, they couple to fulfill the needs of today's consumer: a hard "under" treatment, such as a blind or shade, takes care of the elements of privacy and sun control. A fabric "over" treatment softens the window, adds a splash of color, and provides focus and impetus to the room's design. Finally, a top treatment, such as a cornice or valance, finishes the top and conceals architectural flaws or unsightly drapery hardware.

Below: Golden/green faux linen fabric tops the embroidered ivory geometric fabric panels and frames the beautiful view of the golf course. Fabrics are joined with a fabulous blue, green, and ivory garden bell fringe… all the colors from nature in one trim became the perfect accent for the panels and this room! Coordinating Euro pleated valances in leaf golden/green linen are accented along the bottom with the same fringe. The window treatments create rhythm and cohesiveness in this multi-functional sunroom. Cathi Lloyd, Sylvania, OH. Decorating Den Interiors, decoratingden.com.

Stationary tab top panels with gathered knots hang on a decorative rod over a trimmed roller shade.

Stationary panels over zebra/banded shades hung from acrylic rods and rings. This unique fabric adds texture and dimension. Design by Susan A. Gailani, Gailani Designs Inc. Photography: Richard Lanenga Photography Inc.

The Facts: **Combinations**

Advantages: Offers the functional nature of Modern shades and blinds, coupled with the beauty of fabric; in future years, you could, for example, keep the Modern treatment and have a new soft over-treatment installed, thus changing the entire look of the room without the expense of an entirely new treatment.

Disadvantages: More window treatments equal more money, and a larger space to accommodate. Treatments may not wear at the same rate.

Cost: Multi-layered treatments are the most expensive way of decorating windows. Count on your costs, reaching into the thousands of dollars.

Lifespan: Varying, depending upon the types of treatments being used. Remember that fabric has a lower life expectancy than hard treatments such as blinds. You may find that you must replace one layer, while the other is still perfectly fine.

Most Appropriate Locations: Anywhere that there is space that will accommodate both hard and soft choices. Typically seen most often in dining and living rooms, period-style homes, elaborate sitting rooms, and bedrooms.

Care & Cleaning: Each treatment may require a different type of care. Refer to specific chapters within this book for more specialized information.

Designer Window Fashions

Pleated drapery panels offset classic pole swag and flip-top bell-pull-style ornaments.

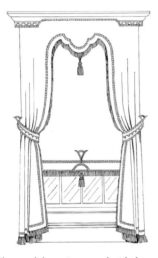

Flat panel draperies topped with decorative wood cornice over trimmed roller shade.

Arched wide Austrian valance with swags, center jabot, and rosettes with French pleated draperies.

The custom drapery and Roman shades in navy and white embroidered fabric pull the look together in this kitchen and family room renovation. Window shadings below provide light

filtration and privacy when needed. Simple, contemporary drapery hardware finishes the look. Valerie Ruddy, Verona, NJ. Decorating Den Interiors, decoratingden.com.

Good to Know: **Combinations**

If you are manipulating the shade or blind treatment regularly, it may not be necessary to have an operational outer soft treatment. Consider stationary panels flanking your window to soften the hard edges of the blinds or shades. Or to minimize light leakage from the sides of the hard window coverings.

- Ensure your hard treatment offers the privacy and sun control you desire; otherwise, your soft treatment should be operational.

- Consider a top treatment to cover the pieces of window hardware needed to hang your other window treatments.

- To change the look of your draperies seasonally, consider a removable drapery swag, which typically attaches to the front of a stationary panel. The easiest way to achieve this is by using Velcro to hang the swags or valances. Perhaps in winter, a lushly fringed velvet swag in a deep cognac tone will add holiday cheer to a patterned drapery panel, while in summer, a small string of silk flowers or an unlined blue silk swag will coordinate and lighten the look.

- While your initial expense may be higher for combination treatments, subsequent redressing of the window may only require a change of fabric while the hard treatment stays.

This page and following page: This traditional living room basks in vibrant colors for this young family. Luxurious fabrics inspired by Oriental designs marry beautifully with velvet and woven textures. Yellow and blue elements balance each other playfully throughout this lovely room. Valerie Ruddy, Decorating Den Interiors, decoraingden.com.

This eye-pleasing straightforward design consists of an inverted box pleated valance with kick pleats. The shutters without tilt bars offer a better view and a more modern motif. Matching shutters with cutouts on the French doors harmonize the overall design. , Sandy Burroughs and Allison Fikejs, Kansas City, MO. Decorating Den Interiors, decoratingden.com. Photography by Jeremy McGraw.

The windows were dressed in a beautiful pearl fabric with a large black and white decorative tape along the edges and hung on a crystal rod. Barbara Elliott and Jennifer Ward Woods, Stone Mountain, GA. Decorating Den Interiors, decoratingden.com.

Above: While shutters provided excellent privacy and light control, they still left the window looking stunted. Hence, the designer added a faux iron transom above the window to give some needed height. The pattern in the faux iron matches the pattern in the drapery fabric. The draperies were also extended so they hung above the transom window. The object of this design was to make the window look taller. Hei di Sowatsky, St. Louis, MO. Decorating Den Interiors, decoratingden.com.

Right: The client requested a chair and a half to fit perfectly in this petite loft area in her home. The space now offers cilantro velvet green seating, beautiful black and white acrylic stools, a custom-built bookcase to showcase her book collection and one-of-a-kind window treatments. The trim selected for the window treatments is the client's favorite: linen, viscose blended oatmeal, and noir-colored curved design. Barbara Elliott and Jennifer Ward Woods, Stone Mountain, GA. Decorating Den Interiors, decoratingden.com.

Right: Open pleated and trimmed swags are pole-mounted on rings. Fringe added to the puddled hem of the pencil pleated drapery adds a touch of drama.

Above: The western exposure dictated that the design needed to cover these windows for the afternoon summer sun. Still, the winter view of the woods necessitated an option to look out the windows, so the designer used Roman shades, which look good whether lowered or raised. The warmth of the natural braided twin blends nicely with the warmth of the stone fireplace. With very little room to mount drapery hardware, panels were attached to boards and installed above the transoms to utilize the full height of the window. Heidi Sowatsky, St. Louis, MO. Decorating Den Interiors.

Opposite page: The original dining room became a secluded home office space. Navy/white drapery on gold rods with acrylic finials adds style for Zoom calls. A sleeper sofa and custom ottomans complement the executive desk and leather swivel chair. A custom wool rug and golf-inspired wall art complete the sophisticated design. Claudia Leah, Naples, FL. Decorating Den Interiors, decoratingden.com

Using most of the existing drapery hardware, the designer simplified the style by eliminating a previous flip-over panel. The new drapery panels were made in an ivory linen-like fabric with metallic embroidery. The new tassel accents at the top are also metallic. The length was shortened to "kiss" the floor rather than puddling on the floor, consistent with the client's desire to "keep it on the lighter side." Decorative brackets were added to the hardware. Decorating Den Interiors, decoratingden.com.

These eye-pleasing window coverings were created by using perfectly matched draperies and flat Roman shades with side banding. A white arched faux grille adds the final touch of creativity. One of my favorite treatments. Design by Cretchen Curk, Cincinnati, OH. Decorating Den Interiors, decoratingden.com.

The Zebra/banded sheer shadings look fabulous in this view window. Note the geometric banding on the leading edge of the two-finger pleated draperies. Adding the white faux wrought iron grille to the arched window was an inspired choice. , Gretchen Curk, Cincinnati, OH. Decorating Den Interiors, decoratingden.com.

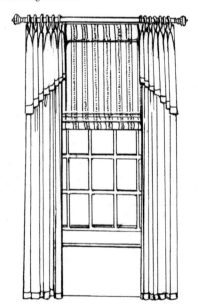

Pinch pleated draperies with asymmetrical flounces over a woven wood blind.

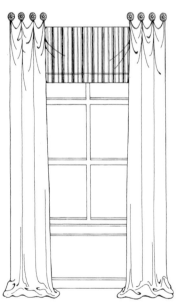

Stationary drapery panels soften the window frame, while the striped Roman shade provides privacy and sun control.

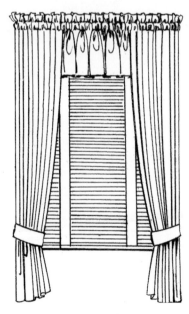

Rod pocket tie-back draperies with center valance over wood blind with fabric tapes.

The designer chose traditional linear pleated style swags and cascades on the familly room windows. This is another great example of mixing design elements and fabrics in the same space: Cinnamon and saffron colors complement each other nicely. Double cascades were used in the center points of the swags, with cascades on each side. This design works well with the window treatments in other rooms and windows of this open-concept home. Sandy Kozar and Rachel Sheridan, Knoxville, TN. Interiors by Decorating Den, decoratingden.com

A combination of shutters and lined window treatments give overnight guests the privacy and light control they need. The two colors in the geometric print fabric for the Roman shades on the French doors and the drapery panels are repeated in the two-toned wood drapery hardware. The geometric pattern in the neutral fabric is created with the embroidered eyelash fringe, giving texture to this multi-layered treatment. The result is a beautiful window treatment that is also functional. Heidi Sowatsky, St. Louis, MO. Decorating Den Interiors, decoratingden.com.

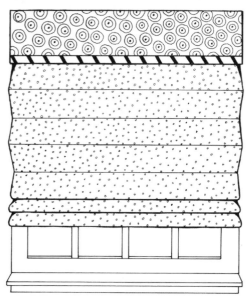

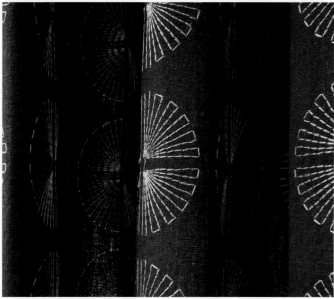

Shutters are an excellent choice for privacy, heat, and light control. Rich dark draperies bring color, pattern, and texture. The minimal black hardware allows the drapery panels to take center stage in this extraordinary and simply stunning design. Valery Huffenus, Asheville, NC. Decorating Den Interiors, decoratingden.com.

Left: Euro-pleated draperies on brass madallions. This design is a great example of sometimes less is more. Why cover the beautiful pallaidian windows?
Better to let them shine and add blinds for privacy and light control. Decorating Den Interiors, decoratingden.com.

Right: Flat panel (non-pleated) draperies with three-inch coordinating banding down the leading edges. The medallions were placed closer together to add fullness to the panels. Add a soft Roman shade in a beautifully coordinated print, creating a designer window fashion! Susan Keefe, C.I.D.

SHADES: MODERN & FABRIC

Alone or as dramatic accompaniment to other window treatments, shades come in all shapes and configurations.

Modern Shades, also known as "hard" shades, such as honeycomb, roller, solar, and woven woods, can fit into awkward areas and inaccessible windows, like skylights, and are sometimes used as unique room dividers.

Fabric Shades, also known as "soft" shades, are clean-edged and neat and can take a back seat to beautiful architectural details when up and out of the way or add stunning emphasis. They are typically an economical alternative to draperies, providing the beauty of fabric with less volume of yardage. In areas where full-length draperies are not practical, shades are ultimately suited.

Left: Fabric Roman shades are the perfect solution for privacy and style because they look good regardless of whether they are up or down. The fabric adds softness to a room full of hard surfaces. The pattern in the window shade fabric reminded the client of the years spent in Singapore. Aqua color was added to the kitchen palette. The designer requested a pattern match from the bottom since the windows were at two different heights. A large-scale pattern was employed to keep harmony in the room. Heidi Sowatsky, St. Louis, MO. Decorating Den Interiors, decoratingden. com.

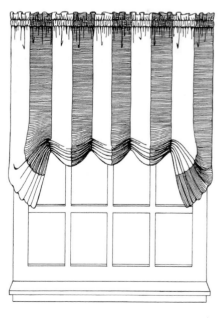

Rod pocket soft specialty shade.

Shades: **Modern Shades**

Today, there are so many shade choices; it's astonishing. From roller shades to honeycomb (cellular) to pleated to woven wood to fabric, there's a shade to fit almost any window. One must first determine whether one wants a Modern shade or a Fabric shade. Modern shades are categorized as pleated, honeycomb, woven wood, sheer shadings, roller, or solar shades. Fabric shades are constructed from drapery fabric or, in rare cases, upholstery fabrics. Look over both sections of this chapter, Modern Shades & Fabrics Shades, to quickly see which style appeals to you. Consider your options, analyze your needs, and plan how you want your new shade to fit into your décor.

These homeowners recently relocated from California and wanted to carry a modern California vibe into their new custom-built home. With a limited budget and expensive tastes, the designer created an exciting family room space that would accommodate their love of entertaining friends and family while providing the comfort of a relaxing space. The modern art, accessories, and dramatic touches gave them a room they could be proud of with the comfort they needed for every day. Lynne Lawson and Laura Outland, Columbia, MD. Decorating Den Interiors, decoratingden.com.

Good to Know: **Modern Shades**
What's right for your design situation? Here's a look at your options

Cellular: see Honeycomb

Sheer Shadings: Most of these products are better known by their brand names, Silhouette®, Luminette®, and Shangri-La®, but also by generic names such as Zebra and Banded, to name a few. In basic terms, they are vanes between which fabric has been suspended. Closed, these products look like regular shades; open, they look like strips of fabric magically levitating across the window. With the treatment in a closed position but with the vanes rotated open, they filter the light, thus allowing more control than other shades.

Honeycomb: Named after the cellular shape of the honeybee comb, honeycomb shades are a flexible, forgiving material that will accommodate unusually shaped windows. With the option of single, double, or triple honeycomb, these cells trap air, making them perfect for homes requiring sound and thermal insulation. They can be installed horizontally or vertically and are available in various material weights, from sheer to complete light blockage. Honeycombs are available in various sizes, from 3⁄8" to three inches.

Matchstick Shade: Like woven wood and grass shades. Horizontally placed sticks of toothpick-thin bamboo are woven together and then folded up in pleats like a hobbled Roman shade or operate as a standard flat shade. They are better used in a sun porch area where the issue of sun filtering, rather than privacy, is most important.

Mesh: Synthetic materials of various weave densities and color options offer a high-tech look. Typically, a roll-up, these shades can be motorized to add to their futuristic appeal.

Pleated: A single layer of sturdy fabric with crisp pleats that fold up like an accordion when raised and offer a slight zigzag look when closed. Fabrics can range from sheer to opaque, and the pleats are usually one to four inches. They are also known as accordion shades.

Roller: Vinyl or fabric, this shade is operated with a spring or clutch system that rolls up into a tube when open. Today, many options exist to add individual design flourishes to the bottom, including lace, fringe, and decorative pulls. Available in sheer, designer light filtering fabrics and blackout. Improvements have been made throughout the years, and the clumsy mechanisms of the past have been replaced with the capability for precise positioning with zero snapback. Decorative valances to hide the top of the roller are now commonplace.

Solar: A spectacular tool to control the sun's harmful rays, solar shades filter and diffuse bright sunlight without sacrificing your view of the outdoors. A downside is that most solar shades are not meant to offer privacy, so they are best used with other treatments, such as draperies if privacy is important to you.

Woven Woods: Beautiful blends of wood, bamboo, reeds, and grasses make woven shades a natural, warm choice. Many require more stacking space than the thinner honeycomb and pleated shades. Banding options add a beautiful finishing touch. Request privacy backing if you want them to do more than filter light. See also Matchstick blinds.

Color-blocked draperies with banding and trim over Zebra/Banded shades. Banded shades have become popular for their smart looks and functionality. Barbara Elliott and Jennifer Ward-Woods, Stone Mountain, Ga. Decorating Den Interiors, decoratingden.com.

Modern Shades: **Sheer Shadings**

Sheer Shadings are an excellent choice for angled windows and French doors. Motorization recommended for high windows. hunterdouglas.com.

I love the bold red color used in this window decor. Add some matching pillows and art, and you have a pleasant modern style, hunterdouglas.com

The Facts: **Modern Shades**

Advantages: Top-down/Bottom-up features in most applications, such as bathrooms and bedrooms, add flexibility. They can work in difficult spaces such as skylights, angled windows, arched windows, and more. The cordless option is usually the best for convenience and safety. Shades are available for inside or outside mountings, and multiple shades can be installed on one headrail.

Disadvantages: Most Modern shades, when closed (except for sheer shadings), cannot manipulate how much light enters the room. Check with your window decorating professional for details. Some arch-top shades are stationary; woven wood shades are not private unless they have a privacy backing.

Cost: It can vary widely depending upon the type of shade selected. Roller shades are still the least expensive type of shade.

Lifespan: Ten years or more. Technology has vastly improved the mechanisms.

Most Appropriate Locations: Just about any window in your home.

Care & Cleaning: Good judgment must be used depending on the type. Always check manufacturers' cleaning suggestions.

Modern Shades: **Woven Woods**

This 1895 home was ready for an update. The original design morphed over the years to include miscellaneous tables, pillows, lamps, and odd accent pieces. It needed to be more cohesive. The designer reupholstered the sofa in a dark charcoal velvet and reupholstered the chair in a rust color performance velvet. The tall chair in the bay was a vintage chair the designer found and had reupholstered in a fun bird fabric. A hand-knotted colorful rug framed the space, new lamps added shape and texture, and original art, both owned and newly purchased vintage pieces, surrounded the room on white walls. A new overhead light fixture and soft blue/green painted ceiling added a pleasant accent. Several period pieces are represented in this room, making the whole room a conversation piece. Suzan Wemlinger, Milwaukee, WI. Decorating Den Interiors, decoratingden.com.

Above: Motorized woven wood shades add texture and interest to the window while providing some light control when needed at certain times of the day without completely limiting the view of the lake. Veronica Simmons, Wixom, MI. Decorating Den Interiors, decoratingden.com.

Modern Shades: **Pleated & Honeycomb**

HunterDouglas.com

Top-down/bottom-up shades are a popular choice for a reason. They provide superior privacy and light control. Duette® Architella® Honeycomb Shade: Fabric: Opalessence™, Color: Silver Sheen, hunterdouglas.com

Modern Shades: **Roller, Solar & Screen Shades**

Hunter Douglas Designer Screen Shades are available in a variety of colors and lifting options. hunterdouglas.com

HunterDouglas.com

Hunter Douglas Designer Roller Shades. Fabric: Giovanni, Color: Silver Dust, hunterdouglas.com

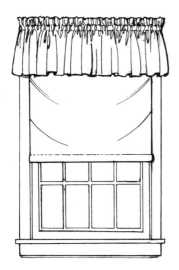

Rod pocket valance over roller shade.

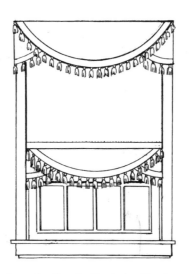

Fringed scalloped roller shade with valance.

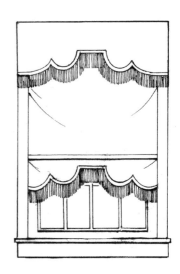

Banded roller shade with valance.

Shades: **Fabric Shades**

Flat Roman shades offer a simple, serene space. Most Roman shades can be ordered in light filtering or room darkening. Deborah Bettcher, West Chester, PA. Decorating Den Interiors, decoratingden.com. Photography by Jon Friedrich.

The Facts: **Fabric Shades**

Advantages: One can use COM (Customer's Own Material) to coordinate with existing fabrics in a room. Decorative fabric offers a softer look and a greater variety of colors and patterns than modern shades. They are recently available in the popular top-down/bottom-up feature.

Disadvantages: Being fabric, this shade is susceptible to environmental factors such as smoke, sunlight, and moisture. Decorative fabric material will break down faster than some modern product shades.

Cost: They are Typically more expensive than a modern shade, as they are often created in a workroom rather than a fabricating facility. Fabric shades can vary greatly in price depending on the style. A flat fold or hobbled Roman shade 36" wide by 42" high can cost $400 or more.

Lifespan: About six to ten years if lined with a quality lining.

Most Appropriate Locations: Any area that needs softening, although drapery fabric, could be better suited for areas with high moisture, sun, or smoke. Lined shades will last much longer and are better for insulation.

Care & Cleaning: As with any fabric-style product, consult with either the workroom that created the treatment or with a professional drapery/shade cleaner.

Simple flat Roman shades in a translucent fabric invite the sunlight indoors and protect from glare when lowered. The royal blue banding is an inspired touch. Jan Bertin and Lorin Petit, Alexandria, VA. Decorating Den Interiors, decoratingden.com. Photography by Jenn Verrier.

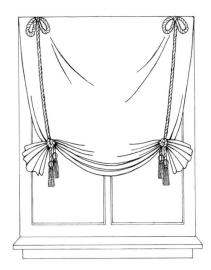

London shade with rope.

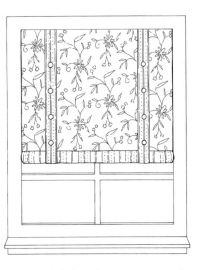

Stagecoach shade with contrast straps and buttons.

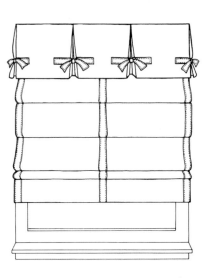

Roman shade with contrast stripes and inverted pleat valance decorated with bows.

Good to know: **Fabric shades**

Fabric shades offer a softer touch to the window, perfect for those rooms where fabric is a must, but draperies may be too much.

Of course, this does not mean that fabric shades can't be used in tandem with draperies or curtains. You will find fabric shades were often used in Victorian interiors, from Art Deco to today's most fashionable interiors. You will find fabric shades in almost every style — from the tailored look of a flat Roman shade to the femininity of a cloud or balloon shade. Add beads, fringe, bows, or ruffles if you want to dress it up.

One important aspect to keep in mind is the lift mechanism and how you will access the cord, be it on the left or right side. Fabric shades can also be motorized if the lift cord is hard to reach (this might be in the case of a window being behind a piece of furniture, for example).

Popular styles of fabric shades are the Austrian, known for its lovely vertical shirring. Roman is the most popular as it can have a pleasant, tailored look. The Balloon/Cloud, both of which are softer looking with plenty of folds. And, finally, Roller shades, which you will also see in a modern style but can also be made of fabric. This shade will draw up from the bottom and into a tight roll. Of course, there are variations in the shades. The London Shade and the Empire are similar to the Cloud/Balloon. Fabric Shades can also have a modern look.

The designer had redone the window treatments before the remodel, so they got a little refresh with new hardware that matched the metal of the lighting. Pink swivel counter-stools (not shown) provide spectator seating as the cooks entertain with their culinary skills. Bohnne Jones, Nashville, TN. Decorating Den Interiors, decoratingden.com.

One of my favorite designs is succulent silk London shades without trim. No need to dress them up. The Shade Store, theshadestore.com.

Above: Take me to the spa, please! Sea and sand are in this pampering visual color palette. Luxury vinyl floors in a driftwood pattern, petal-shaped backsplash, satin brass gold hardware, and faucets nod to contemporary design, with black oval mirrors making a statement. Wall pendant lighting adds a crisp white and gold brass finish, complimenting the black and gold finish chandelier over the sit-down vanity: faux marble tiles and a pebble stone floor. Textured wall covering gives the feel of waves, creating a retreat for this stunning bathroom. Marva Don Card, Fort Denaud, FL. Decorating Den Interiors, decoratingden.com.

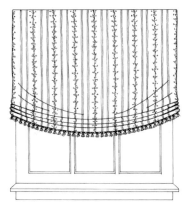

Flat Roman shade with arched trim.

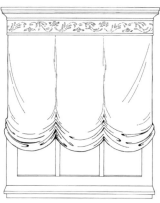

A wood cornice with wallpaper over balloon shade.

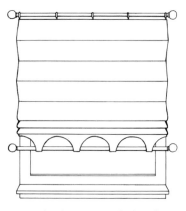

Ring and rod-top Roman shade with inverted tab and rod bottom.

Diverse furniture heights and textures provide depth and interest for intimate piano enjoyment. Custom benches offer extra seating, while soft white Roman shades provide privacy and sound control. Artwork mimicking musical movements adorns the space, complemented by brushed nickel, black accents, and ambient lighting, creating an ideal harmonious musical setting. Kayla Anderson, Dallas, TX. Decorating Den Interiors, decoratingden.com.

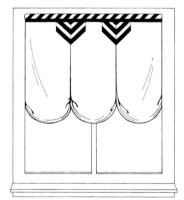

Chevron accents draw the eye toward the window and accompanying balloon shade.

Classic simple lines balloon shade.

A shirred cloud shade exhibits a matching blouson valance.

English turret with leaded glass windows shows three inside mount flat stitched Roman shades, rib on the backside, with black wrapped banding along the edges. Custom made one piece window seat with match-ing pillows. Willow Drapery & Upholstery, Designer: Leigh Anderson, Glenview, IL., willowglenview.com. Pho-tographer: Barry Rustin Photography, Wilmette, IL., barryrustinphotography.com

The outdated brown cabinets were replaced with modern white cabinets with a 10' azure blue painted island. A wall was removed to open the kitchen to the old dining room. Azure blue ceramic tile accents the backsplash. Clear glass and chrome light fixtures highlight this kitchen. Roman shades in blue linen fabric are paired with embroidered panels. Barbara Elliott and Jennifer Ward-Woods, Stone Mountain, GA. Decorating Den Interiors, decoratingden.com.

Good to Know: **Fabric shades**

Austrian: A formal treatment that offers shirred, vertical panels (versus the horizontal panels of the Roman shade). Note that this treatment will tend to pull in on the sides when created improperly. Only use professional drapery workrooms with experience in Austrian shades.

Balloon: Light and airy, this shade can be lined or unlined. A soft, malleable, lightweight fabric is best, in my experience. Completely operational, it resembles its cousin, the cloud valance, when open and also offers the operational capability of providing privacy and protection from the sun when closed. Billowy and lush, this is a beautiful fabric treatment. It closes vertically and is out of the way when open.

Cloud: This fabric shade has a gathered heading that cascades into soft poufs when opened. Like the balloon shade, it can be finished with or without a decorative skirt at the bottom edge.

Roman: This corded shade can have rods set horizontally on the backside of the fabric, which, when raised, form a series of horizontal pleats, usually about four to six inches deep. The beauty of a Roman shade is that it implies the look and feel of drapery, but it raises and lowers horizontally. It can be made with flat or overlapping folds and is not recommended for window applications wider than 60" or longer than 84".

Smocked/Shirred: A traditional Roman shade with a special smocked heading (also called shirring tape) at the top of the shade. It's an elegant style. For the best effect, soft drapery fabrics are suggested.

Coastal dreaming on a cozy sectional with a cuddler and a chaise for relaxing while watching the lake or the game! Console car, swivel stools, and a conversation area with swivel chairs to enjoy refreshments. Lakeside coastal design with seagrass accent tables and decor with every seat inviting you

Color-blocked hobbled Roman shade.

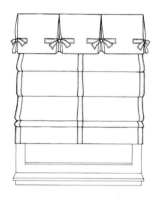

Roman shade with box-pleated valance, ties, and banding.

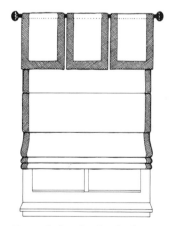

Roman shade with rod pocket flags.

to stay. Marva Don Card, Fort Denaud, FL. Decorating Den Interiors, decoratingden.com

BLINDS

There is something in the structured simplicity of a blind that appeals universally. Neat, compact, and orderly, horizontal and vertical blinds fulfill a multitude of needs with the simple pull of a cord or twist of a wand and, more recently, the push of a button. They usually consist of a headrail system, slats, louvers, or vanes, and, with horizontal blinds, a bottom rail. Blinds can interface with any interior due to the full range of colors, materials, stains, and decorative tapes. Fit them inside the window to align flush with the frame or mount them outside the frame; blinds are infinitely capable of being beautiful and functional.

Left: This large bay window has two-inch real wood blinds for light control and is covered with a delightful geometric fabric. The polished nickel drapery hardware perfectly matches this blue and grey theme. Decorating Den Interiors, decoratingden.com

Two-inch wood blinds with ladder tape under an arched window. The dramatic molding works well with the blinds.

Good to Know: **Blinds**

- Consider cordless blinds for homes with children and pets, which raise and lower with slight pressure applied to the bottom rail. Easy to lift, they provide a sleek, modern look, and the safety issue will never arise again.

- For vibrant colors, consider metal blinds. The color application on metal is bright, tough, and can withstand abuse. They are also available cordless.

- Generally, the smaller the slat, the less light leakage when shut. Micro mini blinds are a great option in areas that require almost total darkness.

- If you aim to enhance architectural details or create a focal point, wood blinds with a quality stained or painted finish will offer a sense of permanence.

- Be sure to select blinds treated with an anti-static finish to alleviate dust build-up.

- Consider vertical blinds if your goal is to enhance the height of a room. The vertical nature will make a low ceiling look higher.

- Vertical blinds allow about 3⁄4" clearance from the floor for ease when traversing. Also, it is important to note that when the vertical blind has been pulled to the side, there will be stack-back — i.e., a small amount of vertically stacked product — that will remain, as there is no headrail for a vertical blind to escape into.

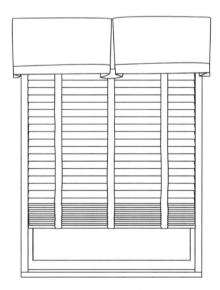

Above: Banded, box pleated valance over wood blinds. Custom rendering by DreamDraper® design software, dreamdraper.com © 2009 Evan Marsh Designs, Inc.

There is something special about the simple, uncluttered lines of wood blinds. Combine those with the ultimate in light and glare control and bringing in a bit of nature to the home, and you will understand the timeless popularity of real wood blinds. hunterdouglas.com

Blinds: **Horizontal**

This client wanted a simple and classic window treatment for this breakfast room that would coordinate with the adjacent great room design. This treatment was designed with a lovely cream linen fabric and gorgeous blue diamond patterned tape with gold edging on either side of the relaxed Roman valances. The result: a simple yet classic design that enhanced and brought together shared spaces. Kirsten Williams, Ft. Worth, TX. Decorating Den Interiors, decoratingden.com.

Horizontal Blinds

Horizontal blinds often come to mind when considering the best method for covering a window because they fulfill many basic requirements and offer a sleek, modern appearance and a low to moderate price point. Easy to acquire, fast turnaround, and various materials and slat sizes make horizontal blinds a perennial favorite. Better yet, their solid construction makes this a window treatment that will last longer than you want.

Matching blinds were used for consistency in the view from outside the house. The designer used a simple treatment with some pizzazz. Neutrals were used throughout the first floor of several rooms, so a linen color fabric was used for the lower portion of the treatment, and "tide" (or teal) was used for the upper portion, tying it together with a beautiful braid. Terry Varner, Port Deposit, MD. Decorating Den Interiors, decoratingden.com.

A light, airy, grey-colored sofa sits on a teal and white rug. A marble-topped cocktail table with a black metal base brings light to the space. An accent chair with a hexagonal-shaped ottoman sits in the corner, coordinating with two soft teal-grey swivel chairs. Grommet-style draperies over white blinds finish this inviting space. Ciera Farley, Nashville, TN. Decorating Den Interiors, decoratingden.com.

The Facts: **Horizontal Blinds**

Advantages: Can control light direction by a simple twist of the slats; will harmonize with just about any soft treatment; can be motorized in a variety of manners; typically a fast turnaround for this kind of product; rout-less (without holes) construction offers the ultimate privacy; hidden brackets and no valance options allow this blind to almost disappear into the inner window frame; cordless operating systems make treatments safer for children and pets

Disadvantages: Rout holes in the center of a blind will allow anyone interested to see inside your home. Be certain you buy a blind with rout holes placed at the back of the slat—or opt for the new "no hole" construction; dust will accumulate, even with a built-in dust repellent; metal blinds can bend and clank against a window when a breeze enters the room.

Cost: An inexpensive vinyl product can cost about $10, but if you are looking for a treatment that will last, expect to spend at least $50 per 30" x 42" window. As always, extras, such as valances and blind materials like wood, faux wood, aluminum, etc., will cause price fluctuations.

Lifespan: Decades

Most Appropriate Locations: Any window will do, although some materials are unsuitable for some areas (such as wood blinds in a bathroom). Also, any treatment near a stove with airborne grease will be difficult to clean. Think about raising your blind fully when cooking to avoid coating the slats, which will, in turn, attract dust.

Care & Cleaning: Most blind slats are anti-static and dust-repellent, though some more than others. Clean the slats with a feather duster to remove the weekly residue accumulation. You can also have blinds cleaned sonically through a takedown, clean, and re-install service that cleans blinds thoroughly without damage or wear.

The sensuous pattern in the ivory and amethyst drapery fabric adds visual interest, complementing the curly velvet sofa (not shown). The draperies were designed to hang just below the crown molding, adding height and elegance while preserving the light, airy feeling in the room. Mary Elliott, Indian Trail, NC. Decorating Den Interiors, decoratingden.com.

Blinds: **Verticals**

Skyline ® Gliding Window Panels and Designer Roller Shades, Fabric/Material: Barista, Color: White Mocha. hunterdouglas.com

Vertical Blinds/Gliding Panels

Neat and elegant vertical blinds can easily cover a large glass expanse, such as a sliding glass door or large picture window. With individual stiffened cloth or vinyl (typically) louvers that can rotate 180 degrees and pull completely out of the way, vertical blinds are a terrific way to obtain coverage similar to that of drapery but with a better capability to control light. Best yet, vertical blinds can strengthen a room's focus with their strong lines and elongated structure. Beautiful colors abound, with embossed prints to fit any décor; custom valances (upholstered and wood, to name a few) to provide a pop of trendy beauty; and the vanes themselves are available from a sheer, translucent material to the hard edge of aluminum. And now, many manufacturers are creating soft fabric verticals (sheer fabric adjoining each vane), which replicate the look of draperies but offer the flexibility of a typical vertical blind.

This is a setting in which vertical fabric panel blinds work perfectly — covering large expanses of glass. Consider opting for a split draw so that you have equal stack-back on either side of the window, versus a large, potentially clumsy stack-back on just one side. .hunterdouglas.com

The Facts: **Vertical Blinds**

Advantages: Can cover large expanses of glass; newer styles hang perfectly straight without any weights or bottom chains; operating systems are now quiet and smooth; some manufacturers boast over 80 colors available; can be motorized in a variety of manners; its elongated structure will augment the height of a room; allows good air circulation; some verticals have the capability of slipping strips of material (such as wallpaper) into the vanes to match a room's décor

Disadvantages: Cheaper PVC vertical blind slats will clank and tangle together; hardware is visible without a headrail (be sure to order one); they're kid magnets (hide and seek has never been more enticing!); perception still puts them in a corporate rather than a residential setting; can be imposing in a room

Cost: Prices can vary depending upon the material selected, but a very simple version, approximately seven feet tall by about five feet wide, will cost around $100.

Lifespan: Decades for premium vertical blinds

Most Appropriate Locations: For areas with great expanses of glass, such as sliding glass doors, tall casement windows, large picture windows, arch-tops, and some angular windows.

Care & Cleaning: Minimum maintenance. Blind slats are now anti-static and dust-repellent, though some more than others. Clean the vanes with a feather duster to remove the weekly residue accumulation. You can also have blinds cleaned sonically through a takedown, clean, and reinstall service that cleans blinds thoroughly with no damage or wear.

Vertical Solutions® Fabric/Material: Afton, Color: White, hunterdouglas.com

Somner® Vertical Blinds, Fabric/Material: Brittmore, Color: Union Square,.hunterdouglas.com

SHUTTERS

A shutter's clean lines and perfect function are a true joy, enhancing any interior with beautiful permanence. Louvers operate smoothly to vary light penetration from full-on bright to almost complete darkness. They offer a warm, traditional appearance and insulate effectively from cold and heat.

The most beautiful wood shutters are constructed with the same attention to detail and loving care as fine furniture. The most ingenious of environmentally friendly faux shutters can withstand the dampest environments. It seems there's nothing that shutters can't do. As someone who owns shuttersw, I can tell you I love how they operate, block heat and light, and look.

Left: The designer started with plantation shutters to help control glare and light. The drapery panels had to accommodate the needed size, and the fabric design needed to be simple and elegant but understated. Hunter Douglass Roman shade cut yardage and Belfast Linen fabric for the draperies. Decorative tape was added above the small folds to accent the bottom of the panels. This is where it would be most visible, but not too much. Kirsch Iron hardware was used to hold the weight of the draperies. Mary Jo Long, Downingtown, PA. Decorating Den Interiors, decoratingden.com.

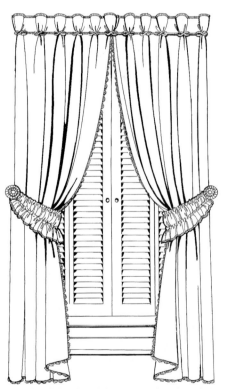

The goblet pleated drapery panels with ruffled fabric tiebacks, a testament to elegance, soften hard shutter panels with a stylish touch.

Today's Shutters

Today, shutters can be found both indoors and out, offering more than just protection from the elements: They offer exceptional beauty, terrific insulation, various light control options, and a life expectancy unmatched by most other window coverings. Plus, you can consider shutters an investment—most are appraised into the value of a home.

And the industry is growing at a rapid pace. Window Fashions Vision, a magazine for window coverings trade professionals, reported that shutters are a billion-dollar industry. Representing approximately 14 percent of the total window-covering market, shutters are showing signs of continued growth and consumer interest. There is a significant expansion in the affluent middle-class market population; homeowners are upgrading to this high-end quality product without question.

Combine shutters with fabric to soften their hard lines or leave them beautifully, distinctively elegant. Comb through the options: plantation, roller, accordion, arch top, Bermuda, and more. With louvers from as little as 3⁄4" to as wide as 5 1⁄2" to suit your needs, there's a shutter waiting to improve your window décor.

This lively and eclectic couple wanted a room that reflected their styles. They wanted draperies but were stuck because one side of the fireplace had windows, and the other was a door they used often in the summer. The starting point of the design was the rug. A muted set of solid blue tones was chosen for the sofa, and two chairs were used to balance the rug. A nice neutral gray was chosen for the drapery panels to offset the brightness of the rug with a nice pop of color from the fabric banding. The tall walls showcased fun art representing the couple's passion for dogs. A large creative chandelier was added to the design to brighten the room, bring the ceiling down, and warm up the atmosphere. Nalini Tandon, Sterling, VA. Decorating Den Interiors, decoratingden.com.

The designer chose a silk-blended rug with luscious, deep jewel tones as the basis for the design. Then, she added a mid-century sofa with abstract accent pillows and a stylish lounge chair. She completes the design with clean lines for the tables and lamps. The artwork was painted by the client's daughter, a professional artist. Marni Sugerman, Riverdale, NY. Decorating Den Interiors, decoratingden.com.

The designer installed textured charcoal wallpaper to make the neutrals pop. The paper had a silver undertone, giving the walls dimension and a deep color. Custom pillows in simple patterns with gray and beige designs were added to the linen sofa and leather chairs. Custom draperies in a linen blend fabric on black wrought iron rods continue the linen look. Adding large mixed-media metal art pieces for color and texture grounded the room with a large wool rug. Mary Jo Lon, Downingtown, PA. Decorating Den Interiors, decoratingden.com.

The Facts: **Wood Shutters**

Advantages: Natural and warm; insulates well; bridges the gap between design styles; high structural integrity; recyclable; can be painted or stained to match any décor; self-squaring frames have eliminated much of the difficulty of installation; prices have dropped due to the product becoming more accessible and available; specialty sizes offer plenty of options.

Disadvantages: Not as effective in areas where water, humidity, and moisture may be a problem, such as bathrooms; wood can warp, crack, or split due to fluctuations in humidity; louvers can accumulate dust quickly if not manipulated/cleaned often; rigid; occasional unpredictable louver quality, especially with painted surfaces; lead time to acquire product can sometimes be lengthy, depending upon the manufacturer.

Cost: Costs will vary depending upon the type of shutter style selected (see "Good to Know" for descriptions), the size of the shutter needed, configurations, and finally, whether it is stained, unstained, or painted. They can also be priced by the square foot or square inch. However, a "normal" double-hung window approximately 30" wide by about 42" high will equate to a shutter somewhere around $200–$400.

Lifespan: Decades

Most Appropriate Locations: Kitchens, living and dining rooms, bedrooms, dens, offices. Do not install in areas of high moisture, such as a bathroom, unless you install faux wood shutters (see "Facts" section on Faux Wood shutters). Interior and exterior applications, although exterior, require regular maintenance.

Care & Cleaning: Minimum maintenance. Use a feather duster or soft cloth to remove dust accumulation between the louvers. Be sure to manipulate the louvers tilted up, then down, to remove all accumulation; washing is not recommended as, despite being sealed, the wood can discolor or warp; vacuuming with a brush attachment is also effective.

3" Plantation shutters without tilt rods are not only practical but also beautiful. The pleated draperies cover the edges of the shutters and add a warm, inviting feeling. Interiors by Decorating Den, Suzanne Christie, Clearwater, FL, decoratingden.com

Combining Smart technology with exquisite design elements, this bathroom makeover embodies luxury and sophistication. From the moment you step into this space, you are greeted by the opulence of the gold chinoiserie wallpaper inspired by the lush views outside the windows. A dazzling crystal chandelier that hangs majestically from the ceiling, casting a warm, enchanting glow as a statement piece that helps set the tone for a luxury experience. A sleek white tub with graceful curves takes center stage, offering a sanctuary of relaxation and the ultimate indulgence. The designer integrated state-

The Facts: **Faux Wood & Vinyl Shutters**

Advantages: Moisture and fire-resistant, these shutters can be used in areas of high moisture; will not warp, crack or split due to environmental introductions such as moisture; can insulate better than wood; environmentally friendly; bridges the gap between design styles; recyclable; vinyl-clad wood shutters have solved the paint/durability problem.

Disadvantages: Louvers can accumulate dust quickly if not manipulated/cleaned often. The cheaper brands may not duplicate the look of a wood product as much as you desire. Shutters are not as flexible when it comes to matching more unusual color tones.

Cost: Costs will vary depending upon the type of shutter style selected (see "Good to Know" for descriptions), the size of the shutter needed, configurations, and finishes. Typically, however, a "normal" double-hung window ap-proximately 30" wide by about 42" high will equate to a shutter somewhere in the area of $150–$500.

Lifespan: Decades

Most Appropriate Locations: Kitchens, bathrooms, living and dining rooms, bedrooms, dens, offices. Interior and exterior applications.

Care & Cleaning: Minimum maintenance. Use a feather duster or soft cloth to remove dust accumulation between the louvers. Be sure to manipulate the louvers tilted up, then down, to remove all accumulation. For more difficult soils, use a soft cloth and a mild soap/water solution; vacuuming with a brush attachment is also effective.

of-the-art features like radiant floor heat, hydrotherapy jets, and wireless temperature control for a personalized, luxurious experience. With the touch of a button, various aspects of the bathing experience are controlled-from adjusting the lighting and the water temperature to controlling the music playlist, every aspect was customized to the client's liking, creating a seamless, relaxing, and convenient environment. Barbara Hayman, Kissimmee FL. Decorating Den Interiors, decoratingden.com.

Good to Know: **Wood Versus Faux Wood**

There are a variety of shutter products on the market today: here's a look.

Metal: Typically used as an exterior product in areas of high hurricane probability, steel shutters are preferred over aluminum for better strength and protection. Due to potentially sharp edges, care should be used for large and heavy installations. Typically, these "hurricane" style shutters are removable in the non-tumultuous "off" seasons and pack together well for storage.

Polycore: An aluminum core is inserted into the center of a solid polymer as it is being extruded. A synthetic material that mimics the look of wood, this material will not chip, fade, or warp over time and can be cleaned with a typical citrus-style product. The aluminum reinforcement allows shutters to be constructed in lengths up to 36" wide, maximizing light control. Its capacity to withstand the hazards moisture makes. This product is capable of being used anywhere in the home.

Polywood®: A synthetic wood substitute (exclusive to Sunburst Shutters), this material is made from natural gas products and is water and fire-resistant. It also withstands peeling, chipping, staining, cracking, bowing, and warping. Easy to clean and care for, Polywood products will work in any home area, particularly in areas of high moisture, such as a bathroom. Environmentally friendly, this product typically comes with a lifetime guarantee.

Thermalite™: A solid, non-toxic, synthetic material, Thermalite is a dense, polymer foam product that greatly resembles wood. Water-resistant and fire retardant, it is stated to be more than two times greater at insulating than wood, and no natural resources are destroyed in its manufacturing process.

Vinyl: Even the most expensive vinyl shutters will still produce less costly products than wood or metal. This is a good thing for those on a budget who can't resist

The right shutter can instantly transform a room into an elegant, feminine retreat. And consider the difficulty of molding fine hardwood into specialty shapes, such as the sunburst arches above these shutters. The purchase of a shutter is considered an upgrade for the home and is frequently added to the value of a property. kirtz.com

the allure of this solid product. Dents and scratches will not show as readily as the color of the louver extends throughout the product. This product works well in wet environments. Limitations include the capability to choose from a wide color range, and vinyl does not look like wood. There is the possibility of warpage, which is lessened with the addition of metal reinforcement in the louvers.

Wood: Attractive and strong, this natural product offers beauty and strength. Its wood grain is unmatched in appearance; all pieces are unique, so if you are looking for one-of-a-kind, natural beauty, wood is your option. Superior construction techniques allow wood panels to accommodate areas much longer and wider than ever. However, if your area is prone to moisture or if you prefer to clean with a water/chemical solution, there may be better choices than wood. As always, wood is recyclable. Typically made from poplar (least expensive), basswood (moderate), or alder (most expensive).

Opposite page: The designer matched the plantation shutters on the windows to match the other windows on the front of the house, then covered them with draperies in a multidimensional fabric. It has a look of liquid silver on the surface with a raised pattern that gives it depth and interest, with a hint of ivory color in the fabric that provides warmth. It was the perfect choice to bring a sense of regal sophistication to the room. The homeowner requested tiebacks, and the antique brass medallions added just the right amount of bling. Donna Rich, Bowie, MD. Decorating Den Interiors, decoratingden.com.

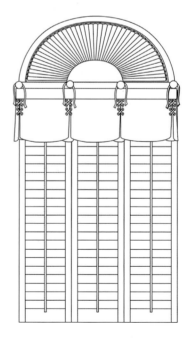

Three-panel shutters under valance with treated arch. DreamDraper® design software, dreamdraper.com © 2009 Evan Marsh Designs, Inc.

Good to Know: **Types of Shutters**

Improperly installed shutters are far too frequent a mistake. Above all else, when installing shutters, ensure the louvers angle up when the shutter is open. This is because (especially when installed outside) driving rain will slough away and run toward the ground rather than into an upward-reaching louver — and then into your home. Also, remember that there are truly no standard window sizes. Each shutter should be made to custom-fit your window. Here are some of the most popular styles:

Accordion: A shutter with a unique, vertical, folding blade system. They are designed to cover a large expanse of glass quickly.

Bahamas (Bermuda): An exterior shutter. It can be crafted from metal, wood, or vinyl. While beautiful, its primary function is security and protection from severe storms. The difference is that this shutter is hinged at the top and opens out from the window like an awning.

Café: A smaller-style shutter covered only the bottom half of a window for a combination of privacy and sunshine.

Eyebrow: A sunburst shutter that is wider than it is high.

Panel: A shutter panel on a track system or a folding shutter, often used to cover a sliding glass door. It can sometimes have fabric, woven wood, or glass inserts. Plantation: The name evokes mansions of the South. Plantation shutters have louvers over two inches wide and four inches wide. Panels are typically installed into the casement of a window.

Roller: Typically installed over a window, it can fit into that area in several ways, including to the wall surrounding the window, into the eave above a window, or in the window reveal. This shutter operates on a mechanism that rolls it into place for security and protection from storms. It can be operated from inside a building. Protection from storms, this shutter operates on a mechanism that rolls it into place. It can be operated from inside the home.

Shutter blinds: Combines the larger louvers of the shutter with the ease of blind operation. Resemble wood blinds.

Storm/Hurricane: For southern U.S. properties and homes extending into the Caribbean, storm shutters are crucial to secure and protect dwellings during inclement weather. Although climate events have shown us that sometimes we are powerless to protect our homes from the magnitude of a violent storm, shutters go a long way to deflect torrential wind and water. While the home may stand after a hurricane, a poorly protected window may allow too much water to enter.

Note that most highly protective shutter systems need time to be fitted and installed effectively. This type of window covering requires planning and a reasonable time frame for installation. Storm shutters are available in many materials, although metal is recommended for dire weather conditions.

Sunburst: Constructed in the shape of an arch, the sunburst pattern is so named due to its design in the form of "rays," all emanating from a central point, usually on the bottom edge of the piece. Specialty sizes are considered an important and necessary part of shutter configurations. Quarter circles, half-circles, tunnels, octagons, ovals, hexagons, and more are available and waiting for your uniquely shaped windows.

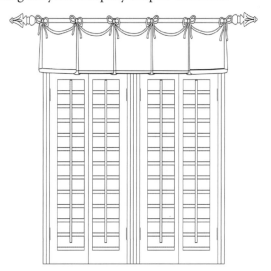

Designer tab top drapery panels over plantation shutters. DreamDraper® design software, dreamdraper.com © 2009 Evan Marsh Designs, Inc.

The designer chose to use purple and create a design incorporating the client's chairs. The master bedroom includes a bold purple accent wall, new hardwood floors, a shag rug, a dramatic modern canopy bed with a grey duvet, and custom-made pillows to tie it all together. Custom-covered benches sit at the end of the bed. Instead of lamps, the designer used pendant lighting over weighty gray cabinets that function as nightstands. The clients especially loved the electric fireplace installed across from their beds and the spa-like feeling it created. Lisa Porter, Dallas, TX. Decorating Den Interiors, decoratingden.com

The windows were covered in white plantation shutters, which worked to keep the sun out but looked unfinished. The designer chose fabrics for the pillows and window treatments that accentuated the client's sofa and chairs. Custom board-mounted side panel draperies kept things simple and were installed over the shutters. Note how effectively board-mounted draperies hide the hardware. Mary Jo Long, Downingtown, PA. Decorating Den Interiors, decoratingden.com

This is a good example of mixing traditional shutters in a modern setting. .graber.com

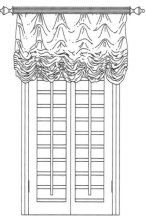

Double-panel shutters under a pole-mounted Austrian shade. DreamDraper® design software, dreamdraper.com © 2009 Evan Marsh Designs, Inc.

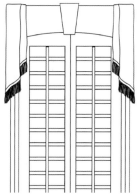

Three paneled shutters with soft valance, center jabot, and pleated cascades. DreamDraper® design software, dreamdraper.com © 2009 Evan Marsh Designs, Inc.

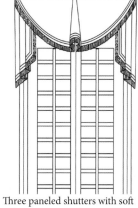

Three paneled shutters with soft valance, swags, and center jabot. DreamDraper® design software, dreamdraper.com © 2009 Evan Marsh Designs, Inc.

Bifold/Accordion shutters are also a good choice for sliding or view windows, hunterdouglas.com

The designer chose an accent wall to align with the client's design preferences and delineate spatial boundaries, particularly emphasizing a mid-century modern aesthetic. This deliberate design decision not only fostered a perception of expansiveness but also enhanced the visual allure of the entire environment, anchoring the room's identity as the family room. To define the dining area within the same space, a vibrant blue accent wall adjacent to the dining table is complemented by featured sconce lighting. Vibrant colors and accent furniture pieces were chosen to complement the custom artwork. Michele Simpson, Dallas, TX. Decorating Den Interiors, decoratingden.com.

This living room is an excellent example of how opposite personalities may come together, with the guidance of an accomplished designer, to create a satisfying space that uniquely reflects the couple's special chemistry. An updated spin on the Art Deco style offered the perfect union of clean lines and graphic drama to suit both parties. Mascarpone white walls highlight the vintage trim, while the contrasting black hue surrounding the fireplace creates a remarkable backdrop to showcase the bold artwork affectionately referred to as "Boss Lady." Deborah Bettcher, West Chester, PA. Decorating Den Interiors, decoratingden.com.

3" Plantation shutters without tilt rods are not only practical but also beautiful. The pleated draperies cover the edges of the shutters and add a warm, inviting feeling. Interiors by Decorating Den, Suzanne Christie, Clearwater, FL, decoratingden.com

Three above: Don't forget that painted shutters can add the spark to make a room light up in a wonderful splash of color. The Shutter Store, theshutterstore.com

Who would have thought a barn door shutter would look perfect in an ultra-modern setting? I love it when designers take a risk and create beautiful, eclectic work. Sunburst Shutters, sunburstshutters.com.

Good to Know: **Shutter Components**

Shutters are typically comprised of the following parts:

1. Rails (including top, divider and bottom): These pieces are structural and range in height from approximately two inches to about 4 1/2" high depending upon the height of the panel and size of the louver.

2. Louvers: Rotating on a pin and connected together by a tilt rod, these individual pieces can vary in size from a typical standard 1 1/4" up to over four inches, depending upon the material used and type of shutter product.

3. Tilt Rod: Connected to each of the individual louvers in the center, the tilt rod controls the light, privacy and ventilation associated with the shutter. Usually moves only up and down.

4. Stiles: The right and left structural pieces, which aid in holding the shutter together. Usually about two inches wide and holds the pins in place that connect to the louver.

These stunning barn door shutters are composed of re-purposed wood and unique wrought iron rail and wheels. Sunburst Shutters, sunburstshutters.com

The value of shutters lies in their extreme durability and classic beauty. Fabric treatments, as well as most shades and blinds, will succumb to normal wear and tear. Shutters can remain in their original high-quality state for decades, if not centuries. Light and privacy control can vary from fully opening them away from the window for a full view, to closing the louvers for an almost light-out effect.

The designers started by choosing a black-and-white color palette, then a geometric black-and-white marble tile for the floors. The ceiling was painted in a black sheen paint. New custom cabinets in a Pure White finish were added to the space for storage. Contemporary black and nickel pulls were added to the cabinet colors. For functional use, the countertops were chosen in a heavy gray, black, and white granite material on top of the washer and dryer. A Roman Shade in cotton fabric with a black and white pattern mounted to the ceiling to extend the room's height. Barbara Elliott and Jennifer Ward-Woods, Stone Mountain, GA. Decorating Den Interiors, decoratingden.com.

Modern black painted shutters without tilt rods work perfectly in this contemporary kitchen. Blinds.com, blinds.com

Solid panel real wood barn door shutters by Sunburst Shutters give the perfect finishing touch to this modern kitchen. Sunburst Shutters, Las Vegas, NV. sunburstshutters.com

Dramatic window accents can be beautiful, but if too much light enters a room, furnishings can take a beating. Consider covering your window with a specialty shaped shutter, which will cut down on glare yet still offer a winning look. Hunter Douglas NewStyle Shutters, hunterdouglas.com

A large bank of shutters covers the French door and windows. Custom rendering by DreamDraper® design software, dreamdraper.com © 2009 Evan Marsh Designs, Inc.

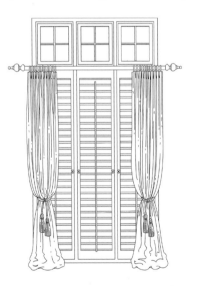

Puddled, blouson tab tops over three-panel shutters. Custom rendering by DreamDraper® design software, dreamdraper.com © 2009 Evan Marsh Designs, Inc.

Designer tab top drapery panels over cafe shutters. DreamDraper® design software, dreamdraper.com © 2009 Evan Marsh Designs, Inc.

Arched shutters are always eye catching. The beauty of these shutters lies in the ability to close the bottom two-thirds of the louvers for privacy. While the top portion allows light in if desired, hunterdouglas.com

Heritance® Bypass Shutters by Hunter Douglas is an excellent choice for a wide space of sliding glass doors, hunterdouglas.com.

Heritance® real wood shutters by Hunter Douglas were the perfect choice for this modern/transitional room. Quality shutters always stay in style and always increase the value of one's home, hunterdouglas.com.

DRAPERY & BEDCOVERINGS

For some, the bedroom is merely a place to sleep. For others, it is a play-room, a reading room, or a quiet place to catch up on work. Yet, no matter how much time one spends in the bedroom, the look and feel of the space are of utmost importance. And thankfully, it is space with options that extend well beyond the decision between draperies, blinds, shutters, or other window coverings. When beginning to design the bedroom, there are infinite starting points. But whether choosing the window, the floor, or the walls, eventually, you will come to the bedcoverings. A well-chosen bedspread can quietly blend with a sophisticated color scheme or quickly become the room's focal point.

Left: It's beautiful when design elements converge to form a personal sanctuary to relax and recharge one's soul. This room exemplifies that concept. Grommet draperies over soft cornices in coordinating fabrics make the statement that a professional decorator designed this room. But it doesn't stop there. Add beautiful custom bedcoverings, a welcoming rug, and accessories, and you have a masterpiece! Decorating Den Interiors, decoratingden.com.

Goblet pleated valance with a trimmed edge; lush draperies and matching bed skirt and pillow.

Today's Draperies & Bed Coverings

Today, the choices have evolved into memory foam, gel, pillow tops, individually wrapped innerspring, waterbeds, air beds, latex mattresses, and finally, my favorite: the adjustable bed.

Since the cost has dropped dramatically over the years, today's bedroom décor often includes coordinating top treatments such as swags, cornices, and an array of bed accents, such as shams, skirts, and headboards. Motifs are often in sophisticated floral prints or light, airy colors that complement the room decor.

Or even a more augmented involvement: a pink and gray gingham bedspread may find its place in a room with a perfectly matched Queen Ann valance, surrounded by simple walls and pale pink pillows.

And when a bedspread is ready to become the centerpiece of a bedroom, the fabric can become as vivacious as reality will allow. Still, bedcoverings should always complement window treatments and other furnishings.

The approach to the design was to choose a soft and luxurious color palette. The bold, Greek key wallpaper created a unique focal point that set as the backdrop for the tall, upholstered bed. Soft, rich bedding in multi-grays and metallic accents added a subtle touch of luxury with a custom, blue-patterned bolster pillow. A vibrant crystal light fixture and crystal-adorned lamps were added to give a touch of bling. The custom drapery panels were designed using fabrics with metallic tape. Crystal window treatment hardware in a black nickel finish was also selected. Comfy and chic accent chairs upholstered in a neutral, textured fabric provided the seating and were paired with a geometric accent table. Kisha Moore, Stone Mountain, GA. Decorating Den Interiors, decoratingden.com.

The centerpiece of the room is an upholstered bed with clipped corners and a tall, tufted headboard. The bed is covered in a luscious denim velvet and accented with pewter nail trim. A soft grey was selected for the wall, and the trim was painted charcoal gray. A crisp white comforter with matched shams was chosen for the bed. Boxed euro shams were fabricated from a teal and navy pattern. Barbara Elliott and Jennifer Ward-Woods, Stone Mountain, GA. Decorating Den Interiors, decoratingden.com.

The stunning bedroom features color-blocked gray and navy silk drapery panels finished with decorative tape. The draperies are hung on decorative chrome drapery hardware with crystal finials. And who would not notice the beautiful round chandelier? Barbara Elliott and Jennifer Ward-Woods, Stone Mountain, GA. Decorating Den Interiors, decoratingden.com.

Three layers of fabric: sheers, silk panels, and a stationary tied-back drapery panel are enhanced by a fourth and fifth layer: a luscious seven-fold board-mounted swag with accompanying tail top treatment. Notice, too, how the treatment also works beautifully as a corona over the bed frame — a sweeping focal point. Photo: Charles Randall

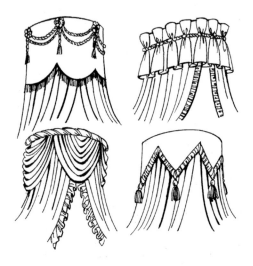

A bed crown can elevate a bedcovering into a fantastic designer ensemble. Above are some various bed crowns.

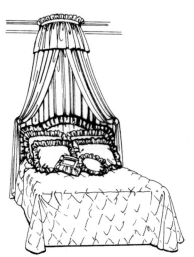

Half-round ruffled valance with fabric draped over holdbacks, upholstered headboard, and throw spread.

A half-round box pleated valance with draped fabric held by rosettes and an upholstered headboard with a throw spread.

The client wanted to transform this bedroom into a light, airy retreat and desired new, softer, brighter window treatments that maintain the same light and privacy as the preexisting treatments. This room has a calm feeling without losing the strong visual impact. Inserting the Tableaux at the top of the windows also allows for privacy sheers without covering the architectural detail of the arches or changing the amount of natural light in the space. Kathy Potts, Forest, VA. Decorating Den Interiors, decoratingden.com.

A gathered valance showcases an elaborate custom wood cornice and bedposts.

A soft scalloped cornice with brush fringe, lush drapery panels, and a gathered dust ruffle, with matching fabric on the bolsters, complete the look.

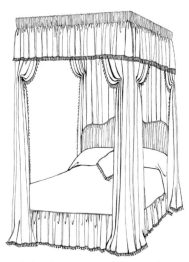

Pencil pleated top treatment with matching side panels and dust ruffle trimmed in tassel fringe.

A perfect example of transitional style. Tone on tone draperies hanging on custom stainless-steel rods and rings. I love the oversized headboard. An excellent example of thinking outside the box. Designed and made by Custom Drapery Workroom Inc., draperyavenue.com

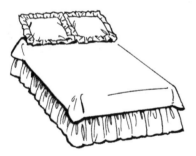

Plain coverlet over shirred dust ruffle.

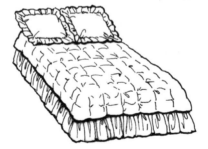

Quilted coverlet over shirred dust ruffle.

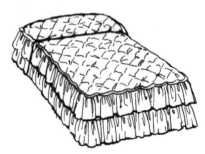

Quilted top with double-shirred drop.

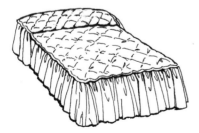

Quilted top with shirred drops.

Plain coverlet with a ruffled skirt.

Bedspread with with two-inch welting.

A perfect example of ultra modern style. Tone on tone draperies hanging on custom stainless-steel rods and rings. I love the white tufted headboard contrasted against a black wall. An excellent example of thinking outside the box. Designed and made by Custom Drapery Workroom Inc., drapery-avenue.com

Goblet pleated drapery panels are attached via rings to decorative rods extending horizontally from the wall. The dust ruffle is an inverted box pleat with a double braid and tassels.

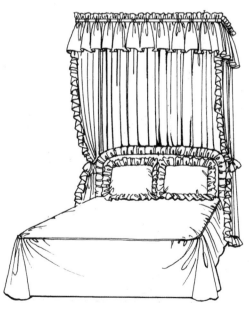

Rod pocket valance with ruffled tiebacks, upholstered headboard, and custom-fitted bedspread.

Asymmetrically curved cornices covered with a small-scale geometric pattern were designed to reiterate the headboard's line. Indigo linen side panels accented with a russet border add softness. The Roman shades of the same blue linen are lined with blackout material, enabling the homeowner to get a restful sleep. Deborah Bettcher, West Chester, PA. Decorating Den Interiors, decoratingden.com.

Above: The client selected intricate, floral wallpaper. The designer warmed it up with custom-painted rattan furniture and simple color-blocked valances with decorative tape to complement the colors. The designer then added adorable throw pillows and simple accessories that gave the room a whimsical feel. Marni Sugerman, Riverdale, NY. Decorating Den Interiors, decoratingden.com.

decoratingden.com

This modern coastal guest bedroom was influenced by the sea-glass tones of the client's wall décor collected during their travels to the beach. The ocean-blue paneled wall accented by white bedding and draperies with blue and palm green accents creates a fresh, serene space where guests can relax and enjoy their stay. Lynne Lawson, Columbia, MD. Decorating Den Interiors, decoratingden.com.

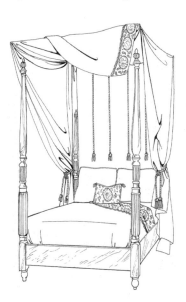

The upholstered headboard fabric matches the gathered bed skirt. Swags, jabots, and drapery panels make this a designer bedcovering ensemble.

Elaborately trimmed fabric is installed just slightly above the bedposts and then wrapped organically. Coordinating pillows and bedding complete this one-of-a-kind design.

This tailored bed ensemble features box pleating and swags on both the top and bottom. Decorative tassels add a designer touch.

DRAPERY HARDWARE & TRIMS

It is with drapery hardware and trims that the customization and individuality of a window treatment begins. A wonderful emphasis for the shape and form of a treatment, trim is at its most effective when placed along the edge or hem of a drapery or curtain, as well as used as a beautiful punctuation to the bottom of a roller shade, or as a decorative tape to soften the hard edges of a wood blind.

Decorative hardware is another means to add emphasis. With many choices in materials — wrought-iron, steel, glass, carved wood, and more — to rings, tieback holders, rods, scarf brackets… your choices are many.

Left: Black iron drapery hardware with large filigree finials was selected for the draperies. The drapery panels are made of satiny scrolled crushed damask fabric in neutral ivory and cream colors. Appealing to the glamorous look of the room, the panels flow and puddle on the floor to provide a softness to the overall look. Between each panel is a soft shimmery valance that mimics an Old World flag with gorgeous large embroidered symbols reminiscent of the European Coats of Arms for members of royalty. The designer chose a gorgeous embroidered fabric tape along the top edge of the entire window treatment, connecting the panels and valances into one very large window treatment. To finish the treatment, embellishments of ribbon ruffled trim in creams and taupes were applied to the bottom edge of the valances. Decorating Den Interiors.

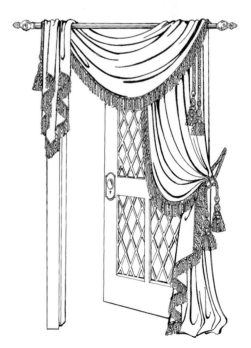

Bullion trimmed swag and cascade is divine.

Today's Drapery Hardware & Trims

Today, the choices are endless. Delicate edging marries beads, feathers, tassels, and tiebacks to form beautiful works of window art. Use a contrasting color for a dramatic look, a tone-on-tone trim for a subtle accent. Place tiebacks according to the "one-third" rule — either one-third from the bottom of the treatment or one-third from the top — but never halfway.

But it is in the application, too, that many a treatment fails. Too much trim will cheapen a treatment; too little will loowk like an effort wasted. If you are in doubt, be sure to talk to your interior design professional. Other than that, enjoy the unique qualities that decorative hardware and trims can bring to your home.

The evening setting sun was addressed by adding an operable lining to the natural woven Roman shades. They provide texture and add to the cultural setting. Charcoal grey embroidered tribal medallion drapery panels hang from oil-rubbed bronze tiebacks. Left and right drapery edges are accented by twine trim with natural wooden beads. The Roman shades have the same trim, adding a rustic yet refined look. When the light filtering privacy shade on the back side is raised, it is possible to see through the woven wood front shade. Erika Lee, Loveland, Oh., decoratingden.com.

The designers created a window treatment in this small room to make it feel larger and taller. They also needed to continue with a design that would complement the ethnic feel designed for the living room. They placed a pair of goblet pleated panels in cream silk fabric on each window, then hung the panels on a decorative rod in black nickel and crystal to the room's ceiling to make it much taller and larger. Then, decorative tape in a black and crème texture was inserted along the edge of each panel to add ethnic flair and softly puddle them on the floor. Now, the room has drapery to complete the exquisite look. Barbara Elliott and Jennifer Ward Woods, Stone Mountain, GA. Decorating Den Interiors, decoratingden.com.

The Facts: **Drapery Hardware & Trims**

Advantages: Adds unique custom elements of individuality to any treatment and enhances a room's visual and aesthetic appeal. The perceived and actual value of a window treatment increases with the addition of decorative hardware and trimmings and, if needed, can provide a focal point.

Disadvantages: Too much trim can overwhelm window treatments. Heavy trims can cause the adorned treatment to sag or stretch. The wrong style of hardware can overwhelm a delicate treatment, and a too-delicate set of hardware can be lost within a heavy, formal treatment.

Cost: This can vary depending on the type and material. Simple rods can be acquired for around $20 but can increase considerably for more ornate detailing and materials; as for trimmings, a simple key tassel starts at about five dollars, but a large, bead-encrusted tassel is upwards of $100 or more.

Lifespan: 10 to 20 Years

Most Appropriate Locations: Decorative hardware and trim are appropriate for any treatment; the trim's placement and style make the difference. Consider a glass bead versus a fringe or fabric-style trim in high-moisture areas.

Care & Cleaning: Check the edges of your window treatment (where it may be handled most frequently) for wear and soiling. Re-sew beads that have come loose and spot-clean according to the manufacturer's directions. Many dry-cleaning services will not guarantee that beads and other embellishments will not come loose with cleaning (such as with a wedding dress)—especially when those trims have been attached with hot glue rather than sewn down.

183

Good to Know:
Passementerie

Passementerie, or trimming, is available in many colors and styles. Here are a few.

Ball fringe: Small balls (such as a pom-pom or even beaded balls) are attached to a flat, raw edge that will be inserted into a seam before it is closed—a more casual look.

Braid: Like gimp (see definition next page), a braid is used primarily to conceal raw edges and seams.

Brush fringe: A more casual look than bullion, the brush fringe looks very similar to its moniker: like a soft, downy brush. When purchased, the brush fringe will have a long strand of protective chain stitches holding the fringe in place. This thread is removed after its installation onto the treatment is complete.

Bullion: Long, twisted lengths of rope form a dense fringe. Usually five inches or longer, it is a lush edging for heavier fabric, such as velvet draperies, although it can be lighter and more casual. It has replaced ruffles as a more popular way to edge treatment.

Button: A decorative accent, typically covered with fabric or woven cord, used to provide a small indentation in an upholstered piece such as a cornice or, more often, a pillow or arm of an upholstered chair.

Cord: Created by twisting or braiding, a cord can be made of various colors and fibers. Typically employed as an edging for upholstery, it can also edge a heavy drapery panel. It has a "lip" to allow ease of attachment in between seams.

Edging: A decorative piece with

The designer used side panels on this large window to retain the beautiful wooded backyard view. A four-width pair gave it enough weight to balance the large expanse of glass. Since the client strongly preferred solid fabric, the designer gave the treatment a wide banding with a distinctive velvet cut pattern on the leading edge. The shimmer in the faux silk fabric coordinated with the

metallic in the wallpaper on the adjacent wall. A long metal rod was used to tie the two panels together but kept the finials very simple since they would be in the room's corners. A neutral paint color was used once the fabrics and wallpaper were selected. Heidi Sowatsky, St. Louis, MO. Decorating Den Interiors, decoratingden.com

one raw edge and one embellished edge.

Eyelash fringe: Named because the short, tiny fringe resembles eyelashes.

Fringe: Available in sizes from about one inch in length to about eighteen inches, fringe is a lighter style of bullion: whereas bullion is more like twisted rope, fringe is more like multiple threads. It can also be a length of delicate tassels, a row of balls, or even beads.

Gimp: A thin, woven braid typically used to cover seams or to mask upholstery tacks or staples. Usually silk or metallic, it is finished on both edges and can be sewn on or glued.

Key tassel: A small, decorative tassel used for accentuating.

Lip cord: A decorative cord to which a narrow piece of fabric (the lip) has been attached. That fabric is slid into an open area (to be seamed) during the construction of a drapery. When the seam is stitched, the cord conceals the seamed area.

Loop fringe: Like brush fringe, only the fringe loops back into the final or lip cord rather than being cut at the bottom.

Piping: A thin cord covered in a fabric used primarily to cover seams or finish edges of furniture or finish cornice boxes.

Rickrack: Rickrack is a flat piece of braided trim shaped like a zigzag. It is used as a decorative element in clothes or curtains.

Rosette: A detailing piece of fabric sewn to look like a rose or other design. It resembles a flower and can be quite large at the top of drapery or quite small, such as when used to dot the side of an upholstered chair. See photo examples in this chapter and on-page.

Tassel: Consisting of three main parts: the cord (used to suspend the tassel), the top (holds the fringe in place, can also be called a finial), and the skirt (the fringe that hangs from inside the top of the piece), a tassel can range from very simple. See photo examples in this chapter.

1127A1-20 Need caption and designer

Drapery Hardware

While hardware falls into two categories, the visual and the non-visual, you can't have a traversing window treatment without it. Beautiful hardware makes your window treatment unique and eye-catching. See many photo examples in this chapter and the Draperies and Curtains chapter.

Baton: A long wand made of wood, metal, or acrylic that attaches to a drapery's top edge. Its main function is to offer an easy way to traverse draperies back and forth without touching (and thus, possibly soiling) the fabric. Usually, it is hidden in the folds of the draperies when opened and hangs behind the drapery rather than in front. Exception: Hotels usually place the baton outside the drapery master carrier to ensure the quest sees the wand.

Bracket: An indiscrete piece of hardware. Many newer brackets are meant to be seen. Brackets hold the drapery rods in place. If decorative, they are visible, such as at the end of poles, as a point of emphasis, but most often, brackets are hardware best left hidden.

Final: Decorative hardware attached to the very ends of decorative rods, adding beauty and keeping the drapery from sliding off the end. Many photo examples are shown in this chapter and the Draperies & Curtains chapter.

Holdback: A piece of hardware placed about one-third to midway between the top and bottom of a window, used to hold draperies back to either side and typically used in conjunction with a tieback.

Ring: The ring has different uses. It is a circular hardware piece available in many different sizes and materials. When small, it is used in conjunction with a rod and helps the drapery traverse—used in combination with a drapery hook, which is hidden inside of a pinch pleat at the top of the drapery, for example. When used in a larger format, it can become a bracket used to sling a scarf treatment through or offer some

Gathered flip-topper panels in flowing floral fabric color blocked moire blue. Tiebacks out of decorative four-inch wide floral fabric. Accessories in blue-greens, teal, and white. Hardware acrylic rod with Murano glass finials. Diana Apgar, Middletown, OH. Decorating Den Interiors, decoratingden.com.

containment for holding a part of the drapery. The larger format ring is stationary.

Rod: A straight piece of drapery hardware usually made of wood, polymer, or a metal such as wrought iron or steel suspended between two points using brackets or rod end holders. Attached at the top of a window frame or even further up at or on the ceiling, the drapery rod is the primary piece of hardware used to suspend a window treatment.

Another example of 'thinking outside of the box." Using two different hardware styles in the same room? It works perfectly. Custom window treatments are just that—custom. The only limit is the designer's and client's imagination. Decorating Den Interiors, decoratingden.com.

Decorating Den Interiors

Various tassels and trims.

Trims & Tassels

- Too much passementerie: too many beads, too many rows of fringe, too many tiebacks, gimp, braids, and more, can make a mess of a beautiful treatment. Choose your trims sparingly, and you will be satisfied.

- Not all passementerie is formal. The wide variety of trims makes it possible to accentuate in countless ways: masculine, exotic, regal, fanciful, pretty, modern. The type of trim you select can set or enhance a mood and tie together disparate elements.

- Plan your trims carefully. A good rule is to choose a trim color that complements the main fabric and is **consistent with its style and treatment shape.** Tone-on-tone coloration, however, is also very beautiful in its subtlety.

Asymmetrical pole-mounted swags.

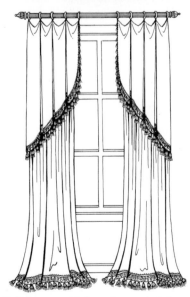

Cuffed asymmetrical panels over pleated puddled draperies.

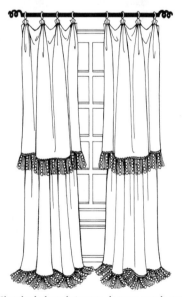

Slouched pleated ring top drapery panels are doubled up to draw the eye to the center of the treatment, showcasing intricate fringe and bead trim.

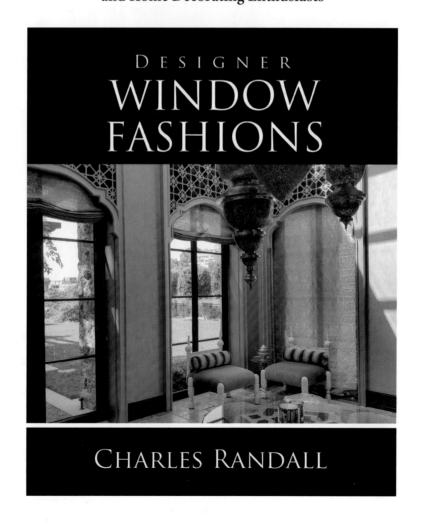